Visual Reference Basics

Microsoft®
Office 2000

Marni Ayers Brady
Karl Schwartz
Diana Rain
Maria Reid

Acknowledgements

Managing Editor
Jennifer Frew

English Editor
Jacinta O'Halloran

Technical Editors
Frank Dauenhauer
Howard Peterson
John Ralston
Diana Ranken

Layout and Design
Elsa Johannesson

Cover Design
Amy Capuano

Cat No: G40
ISBN No: 1-56243-628-7

First DDC Publishing, Inc. Printing
10   9   8   7   6   5   4   3   2

Printed in the United States of America.

Table of Contents

Integration *235*

Index *243*

Introduction

DDC's Visual Reference Basics series is designed to help you make the most of your software. These books are equally useful as instruction manuals or as desktop reference guides for the experienced user. With illustrations and clear explanations of every step involved, they make even complex processes easy to understand and follow.

The most distinctive feature of this series is its extensive use of visuals. Buttons, toolbars, screens, and commands are all illustrated so that there is never any doubt that you are performing the right actions. Most information can be understood at a glance, without a lot of reading through dense and complicated instructions. With Visual Reference Basics, you learn what you need to know quickly and easily.

This book contains one hundred functions essential for optimal use of Microsoft Office 2000. Each section covers the most commonly performed functions and features.

The Visual Reference Basics series is an informative and convenient way to acquaint yourself with the capabilities of Microsoft Office 2000.

Word

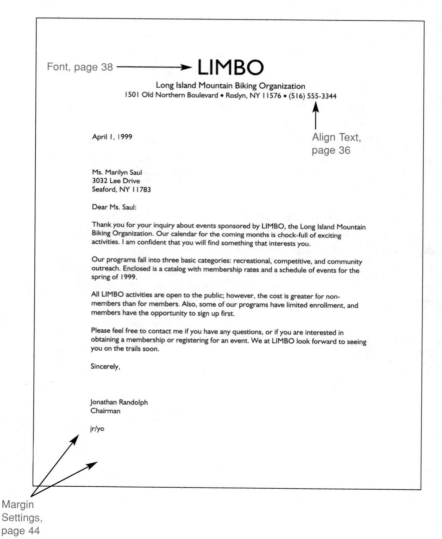

Font, page 38 ——————→ **LIMBO**

Long Island Mountain Biking Organization
1501 Old Northern Boulevard • Roslyn, NY 11576 • (516) 555-3344

April 1, 1999

Align Text,
page 36

Ms. Marilyn Saul
3032 Lee Drive
Seaford, NY 11783

Dear Ms. Saul:

Thank you for your inquiry about events sponsored by LIMBO, the Long Island Mountain Biking Organization. Our calendar for the coming months is chock-full of exciting activities. I am confident that you will find something that interests you.

Our programs fall into three basic categories: recreational, competitive, and community outreach. Enclosed is a catalog with membership rates and a schedule of events for the spring of 1999.

All LIMBO activities are open to the public; however, the cost is greater for non-members than for members. Also, some of our programs have limited enrollment, and members have the opportunity to sign up first.

Please feel free to contact me if you have any questions, or if you are interested in obtaining a membership or registering for an event. We at LIMBO look forward to seeing you on the trails soon.

Sincerely,

Jonathan Randolph
Chairman

jr/yo

Margin
Settings,
page 44

CREATIVE ADVANCES IN COMPUTER DESIGN

Chicago, IL   October

Welcome to the *Creative Advances in Computer Design* Symposium.

The agenda is chock full of forums, lectures, and roundtables which you are sure to find exciting and informative.

If you have any questions about the symposium, the agenda, or extracurricular activities please contact Karin Paolo, Events Coordinator.

Create a Table, page 54

SYMPOSIUM AGENDA

	Sunday	Monday	Tuesday	Wednesday	Thursday	Friday
7:30 - 8:45 a.m.		Continental Breakfast				
9:00 - 11:30 a.m.		Seminar: Using Color in Web Page Design	Roundtable: Marketing on the Web	Workshop: Web Page Animation	Q & A with Sarah Ching, President Expose, Inc.	Check Out by 11:30
11:45 a.m. - 1:15 p.m.		Lunch		Lunch and Keynote Address.	Lunch	
1:30 - 3:00 p.m.	Check in and registration	Roundtable: Is there such a thing as too many links?	Seminar: Interactive Web Pages	Speaker TBA	Workshop: Designing Web Pages with MS Word.	
3:00 - 5:00 p.m.		Open				
5:15 - 6:30 p.m.		Cocktails with the Sponsors				
7:00 p.m.		Dinner				

Visual Index

Excel

Select cells, columns, and rows,
page 62

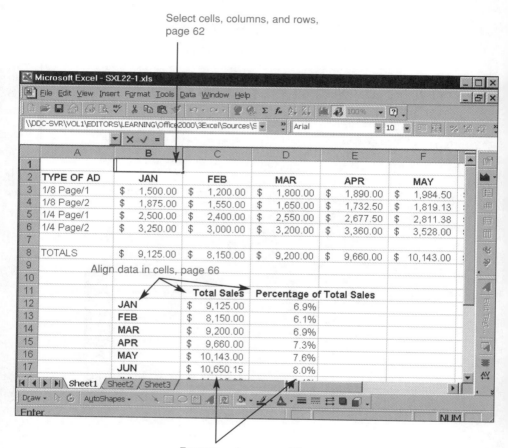

Align data in cells, page 66

Format numbers, page 78

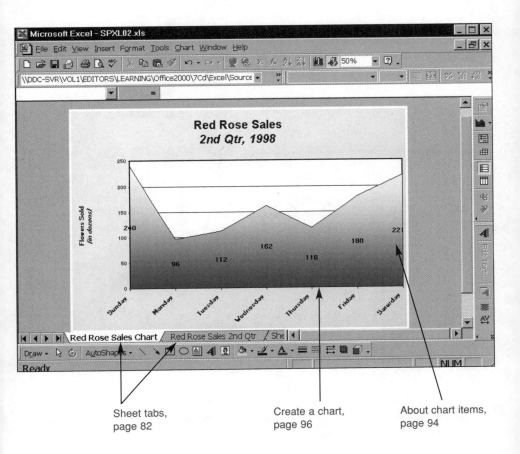

Sheet tabs,
page 82

Create a chart,
page 96

About chart items,
page 94

Visual Index

(continued)

Access

Create a database using a wizard,
page 106

Create a table using a wizard,
page 114

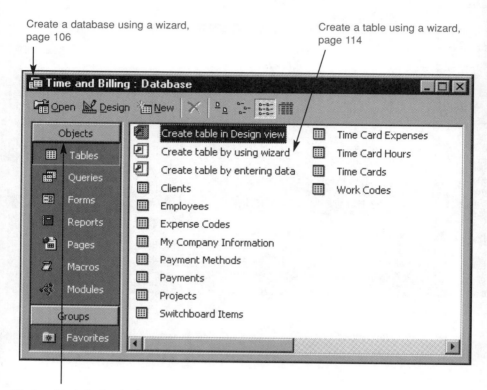

Display objects in the database wizard,
page 100

Product Name	Category	Unit Price	Units In Stock
Chai	Beverages	$18.00	39
Chang	Beverages	$19.00	17
Aniseed Syrup	Condiments	$10.00	13
Chef Anton's Cajun Seasoning	Condiments	$22.00	53
Chef Anton's Gumbo Mix	Condiments	$21.35	0
Grandma's Boysenberry Spread	Condiments	$25.00	120
Uncle Bob's Organic Dried Pears	Produce	$30.00	15
Northwoods Cranberry Sauce	Condiments	$40.00	6
Mishi Kobe Niku	Meat/Poultry	$97.00	29
Ikura	Seafood	$31.00	31
Queso Cabrales	Dairy Products	$21.00	22
Queso Manchego La Pastora	Dairy Products	$38.00	86
Konbu	Seafood	$6.00	24
Tofu	Produce	$23.25	35
Genen Shouyu	Condiments	$15.50	39
Pavlova	Confections	$17.45	29
Alice Mutton	Meat/Poultry	$39.00	0
Carnarvon Tigers	Seafood	$62.50	42
Teatime Chocolate Biscuits	Confections	$9.20	25
Sir Rodney's Marmalade	Confections	$81.00	40
Sir Rodney's Scones	Confections	$10.00	
Gustaf's Knäckebröd			
Tunnbröd			
Guaraná Fantástica			

To show only particular records, Filter Records in a Datasheet or Form, page 126

Product Name	Category	Unit Price	Units In Stock
Aniseed Syrup	Condiments	$10.00	13
Chef Anton's Cajun Seasoning	Condiments	$22.00	53
Chef Anton's Gumbo Mix	Condiments	$21.35	0
Grandma's Boysenberry Spread	Condiments	$25.00	120
Northwoods Cranberry Sauce	Condiments	$40.00	6
Genen Shouyu	Condiments	$15.50	39
Gula Malacca	Condiments	$19.45	27
Sirop d'érable	Condiments	$28.50	113
Vegie-spread	Condiments	$43.90	24
Louisiana Fiery Hot Pepper Sauce	Condiments	$21.05	76
Louisiana Hot Spiced Okra	Condiments	$17.00	4
Original Frankfurter grüne Soße	Condiments	$13.00	32

This example filters out all records that do not have Condiments in the Category field.

Visual Index

PowerPoint

Transitions,
page 186

Slide Sorter view,
page 158

Group objects,
page 170

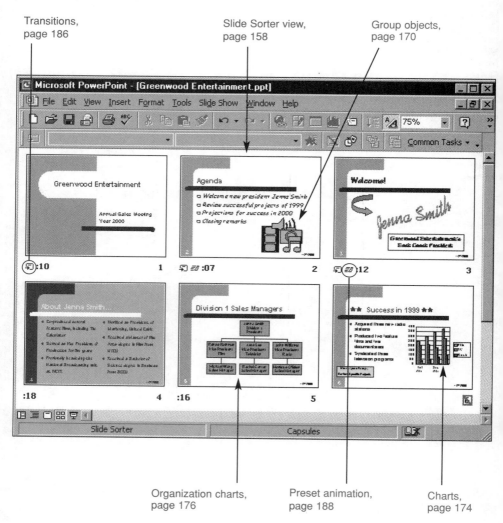

Organization charts,
page 176

Preset animation,
page 188

Charts,
page 174

Design template,
page 152

Background,
page 160

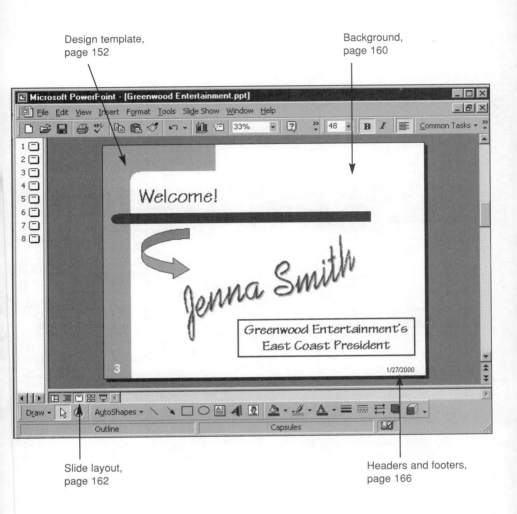

Slide layout,
page 162

Headers and footers,
page 166

Visual Index

(continued)

Outlook

Create a recurring appointment, page 202

Add holidays, page 204   Create an appointment, page 200

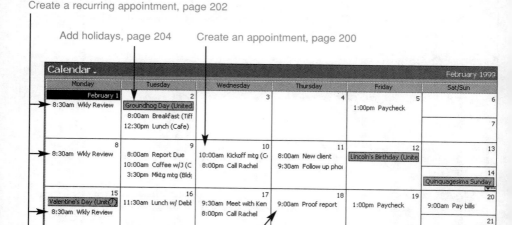

Schedule time for a task, page 232

Outlook Today view gathers information from various
Outlook components into a single window, page 198.

Add holidays to your Calendar, page 204

Monday, November 30, 1998

Customize Outlook Today ...

Calendar

Today

Multi-day event	First Sunday of Advent (Christian Religious Holidays)
Multi-day event	First Sunday of Advent (Christian Religious Holidays)
▶ 4:30 PM - 5:00 PM	Wkly Review

Tuesday

8:00 AM - 9:00 AM	Breakfast (Tiffany's)
3:00 PM - 4:30 PM	Status Meeting (Conf Room)

Wednesday

8:00 PM - 8:15 PM	Call Rachel

Thursday

10:00 AM - 10:30 AM	Kickoff Mtg (Atrium)

Messages

Inbox	13
Drafts	2
Outbox	0

Tasks

- ☐ Ch09 Idx (6/3/99)
- ☐ ! Chapter 1 edit (6/2/99)
- ☐ Proof sales report (6/1/99)
- ☐ Chapter 2 Edit (6/1/99)
- ☐ Proof status report (5/28/99)
- ☐ Proof product status report (5/21/99)
- ☐ CH014 Idx (1/20/99)
- ☐ Ch08 Idx (6/10/98)

Create an appointment, page 200

Create a task, page 232

XV

Basics

Because the Microsoft Office suite is several tools packaged together, you will find that many of the functions work the same way. In Basics, several of the features common to Word, Excel, Access, PowerPoint, and Outlook are illustrated. As you become proficient in one Office application, you will find that those skills become applicable in the other applications as well.

Set Office Assistant Options

The Office Assistant is an automated and interactive helper that pops up on-screen when you perform certain actions. It is available in all Microsoft Office 2000 applications and offers a variety of help options. Use the following procedures to set and control your Office Assistant. Use them also to choose a different Office Assistant character.

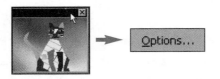

Notes:

- You can turn off all options so that the Office Assistant never starts automatically. To start the Office Assistant manually, click the **Office Assistant** button .

1 Click the **Office Assistant** button 🔲 to open the Office Assistant window if necessary.

2 Click the **Options** tab to display the Office Assistant dialog box.

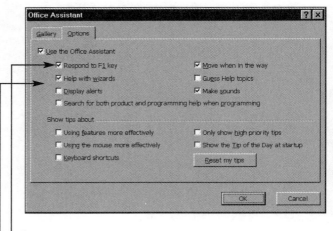

3 Set **Respond to F1 key** option:

Select the option if you want to start the Office Assistant when you press **F1**.

OR

Deselect the option if you want to open the Help Contents and Index when you press **F1**.

4 Select or deselect other **Assistant capabilities** options as follows:

- **Help with wizards**. Displays the Assistant when you select a command that starts a wizard. For example, importing an address book starts the Import Wizard.
- **Display alerts**. Displays general messages about actions. These are often troubleshooting tips.

- **Search for both product and programming help when programming**. Displays both Visual Basic and user help topics when you work in a Visual Basic module. If not selected, displays only programming help topics.
- **Move when in the way**. Shrinks the Assistant when you have not asked for help in five minutes and moves the Assistant window so that it is not on top of open dialog boxes.
- **Guess help topics**. Starts context-sensitive Assistant help. The Assistant tracks your actions and displays a list of help topics based on what you are doing when you ask for help. For example, if you have an appointment open when you click the Assistant to get help, the balloon lists a number of help topics on entering appointments.
- **Make sounds**. Enables or disables sound effects if you have a sound card.

5 Select or deselect **Show tips about** options to specify the kinds of tips you would like the Office Assistant to display.

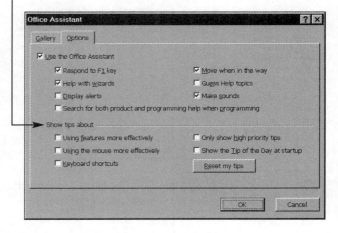

- **Only show high priority tips**. Deselect if the Assistant displays tips that are not useful.
- **Show the Tip of the Day at startup**. Displays an Outlook tip each time you start Outlook.
- **Reset my tips**. Outlook remembers which tips you have viewed and will not redisplay them. Click this button to start redisplaying tips that you have already seen.

7 To choose a different character, click the **Gallery** tab.

8 Click **OK** OK .

3

Toolbars

Unlike previous versions of Office, the Standard and Formatting toolbars now appear on one row and are personalized like menus. The first time Office applications are launched, the toolbars display the most basic options. As you use the applications, they automatically replace those buttons that you do not use with buttons you have recently used.

Notes:

• For some steps in this book, you will probably need to access hidden buttons with the **More Buttons** arrows (see *Access a Hidden Button*).

View Toolbars on Two Rows

1 Click **Tools**, **Customize**. The Customize dialog box appears.

2 Click **Options** tab.

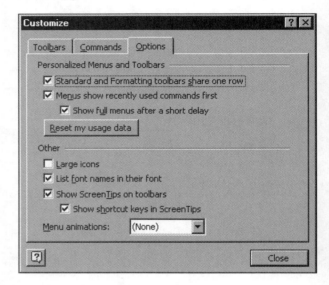

3 Click **Standard and Formatting toolbars share one row** to deselect it.

4 Click the **Close** button | Close |.

   To drag Formatting toolbar below Standard toolbar:

   a. Point to the **Formatting toolbar** sizing handle ▯.

   Pointer changes to ⬌.

   b Drag **Formatting** toolbar below **Standard** toolbar.

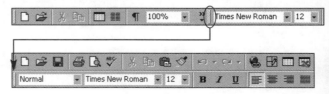

Access a Hidden Button

1   Click **More Buttons** arrow 💠 on toolbar containing button.

The **More Buttons** arrow may look like ▾ or ▼ depending on the location of the toolbar.

2   Click button to use.

Add/Remove a Toolbar Button

1   Click **More Buttons** arrow 💠 on toolbar containing button.

The **More Buttons** arrow may look like ▾ or ▼ depending on the location of the toolbar.

2   Click **Add or Remove Buttons**.

3   Click the button you want to add or remove.

If button is not displayed:

a. Select **Customize**. The Customize dialog box appears.

b. Click **Commands** tab.

c. Select category. The commands and buttons grouped under the selected category appear in the **Commands** list box.

d. Drag button into position on toolbar to add button.
   OR
   Drag button off the toolbar to remove button.

e. Click the **Close** button ▕ Close ▏.

Display/Hide Toolbar

1   Click **View**, **Toolbars**.

OR

Right-click on any toolbar.

2   Select toolbar to display/remove. Currently displayed toolbars are marked with a check mark.

Toolbar Options

1 Click **Tools**, **Customize**.

2 Click **Options** tab.

3 Select desired toolbar options:
- **Large icons** to increase toolbar button size.
- **Show ScreenTips on toolbars**. ScreenTips display pop-up names of buttons.

- **Show shortcut keys in ScreenTips**.

4 Click the **Close** button.

Move Toolbar

1 Point to toolbar sizing handle. Pointer changes to ✛.

2 Drag toolbar to new location.

Dialog Box Elements

An ellipsis (…) following a menu item indicates that a dialog box will open. Dialog boxes may contain the following elements.

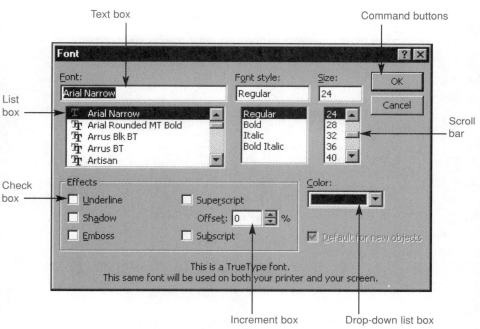

Text box — Command buttons

List box

Scroll bar

Check box

Increment box — Drop-down list box

Command buttons	Carry out actions described in the button's name.
Check box	Provides a space where you can select or deselect an option.
Drop-down list box	Provides a drop-down arrow you can click to select an item from the list.
Increment box (or Spin box)	Provides a space for typing a value. Increment arrows let you select a value with the mouse.
List box	Displays a list of items from which selections can be made.
Text box	Provides a space for typing in information
Scroll bar	Provides scroll arrows and a scroll box that you can use to show hiddens items in a list.
Radio buttons	Circle-shaped buttons that mark options in a set.
Named tabs	Found at the top of some dialog boxes and categorize options by the tab's name.

Menus

The personalized menus in the latest version of Office put the features you use most frequently within easy reach. The first time an Office application is launched, the personalized menus display the most basic options. The advanced menu options are hidden, and may be accessed at any time. As you use Office applications, the basic options that you do not regularly use are replaced by features that you do employ.

Display Full Menu

Display all menu options of a personalized menu.

Double-click the menu to open.

OR

1   Click the menu to open.

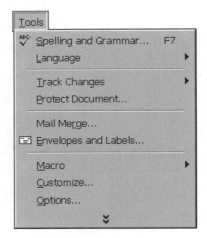

2   Point to the **Expand Arrows** button

.

OR

Leave menu open for three seconds. The full menu is displayed.

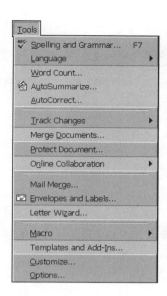

Permanently Display All Full Menus

1 Click **Tools**, **Customize**.

2 Click **Options** tab.

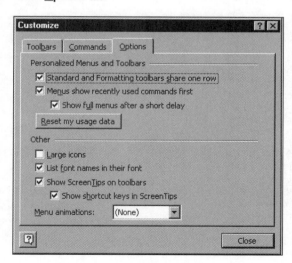

3 Click **Menus show recently used commands first** to deselect it.

Save

Until a document has been saved to a disk, any changes that have been made to it exist only in the computer's temporary RAM.
NOTE: With Outlook and Access, only the Save As option is available. Incremental tasks are saved to your hard drive as they are completed.

Notes:

- The keyboard shortcut for saving a document is **Ctrl + S**.

- New documents, as well as any changes made to an open document, are stored in the computer's temporary RAM (Random Access Memory) until the document, or changes to the document, are saved.

- If a power outage or system crash occurs, anything in RAM will be lost. To guard against such disaster, make it a habit to periodically save all open documents.

- A document's default name (Document 1, Document 2, etc.) can be changed when you save it for the first time.

1 Click **File**, **Save** to display the Save As dialog box.

OR

Click the **Save** button.

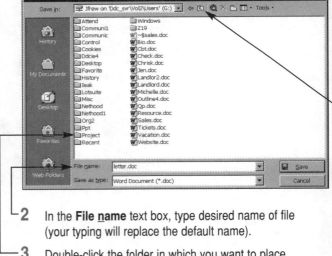

2 In the **File name** text box, type desired name of file (your typing will replace the default name).

3 Double-click the folder in which you want to place the document.

4 Click the **Up One Level** button to display the folders stored along with the folder currently displayed in the **Save in** text box.

- The first time you save a document, a Save As operation is performed by the computer. This enables you to name the document for the first time and to indicate where you wish to save it. Each additional Save will simply save the most recent changes to the current document. The Save As dialog box will not reappear unless you choose Save As in place of Save.

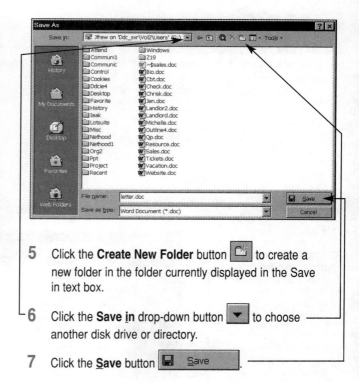

5 Click the **Create New Folder** button to create a new folder in the folder currently displayed in the Save in text box.

6 Click the **Save in** drop-down button to choose another disk drive or directory.

7 Click the **Save** button.

Save As

The Save As command is used to save an additional copy of a document with a different name or to a different directory or disk than the original document.

1   Click **File**, **Save As** to display the Save As dialog box.

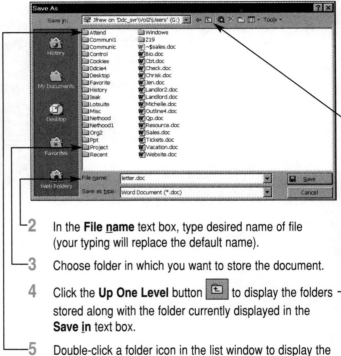

2   In the **File name** text box, type desired name of file (your typing will replace the default name).

3   Choose folder in which you want to store the document.

4   Click the **Up One Level** button 🔼 to display the folders stored along with the folder currently displayed in the **Save in** text box.

5   Double-click a folder icon in the list window to display the contents of that folder.

12

6 Click the **Look in Favorites** button 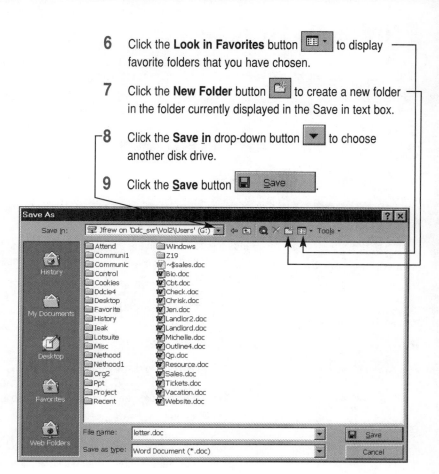 to display favorite folders that you have chosen.

7 Click the **New Folder** button to create a new folder in the folder currently displayed in the Save in text box.

8 Click the **Save in** drop-down button to choose another disk drive.

9 Click the **Save** button.

Print a Document

The Print command sends the currently active document to the printer. Until they are printed, print jobs are stored in Print Manager. The Print dialog box for each application may vary slightly.

Notes:

- The keyboard shortcut for printing a document is **Ctrl + P**.

- When documents are printing, a small icon appears on the taskbar at the bottom right corner of the screen.

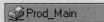

- What your actual printer button will say depends on the type of printer you have, and what your printer name may be.

- Double-click the icon to open the printer dialog box. There you will see a list of pending print jobs, which you can rearrange or delete.

Toolbar

Sends the document in the active window directly to the printer using the default printer settings. The Dialog Box options are not presented.

- Click the **Print** button .

Dialog Box

1   Click **File**, **Print** to display the Print dialog box.

2   Click the **Name** drop down button ▼ to choose the desired printer.

3   Click the **Properties** button Properties to change printer properties, such as print quality (options will vary depending on your printer).

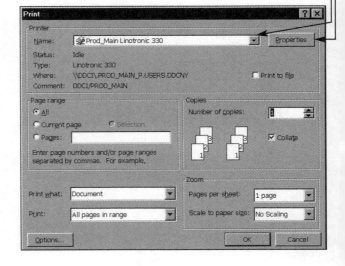

14

- You can print different page range combinations in a document. From the Print dialog box, click to select a page range:

  All to print all the pages of the document.

  Current page to print the page on which the insertion point is resting.

  Selection to print currently selected text and graphics (must have been selected before dialog box was opened).

  Pages to print desired page numbers (use a hyphen to specify a page range: 5-10; or use a comma to separate individual pages: 5,10).

- PowerPoint enables you to print slides, outlines, handouts or notes pages.

4 Check a desired **Page range** to print (see options in note box to the right).

5 Click **Number of copies** and type the desired number of copies to print.

6 Click the **Print** drop-down button to print odd or even pages only.

7 Click **OK**.

Word

Microsoft Office's word-processing application is an extremely versatile program that allows you to create both visually exciting documents that can contain drawings, tables, charts, as well as basic correspondence and reports. This book will familiarize you with creating, formatting, and printing Word documents, as well as with various functions that will help you to get the most out of Word 2000.

Open a Document

Open a document that has been saved on a disk, your hard drive, or, if you're on a network, a network drive. Open a document to edit it.

Notes:

- The keyboard shortcut to open a document is **Ctrl + O**.

- When you open a file of another format, such as a WordPerfect file or a file from a previous version of Word, Word will attempt to automatically convert the file to Word 2000 format.

- Opening a file automatically creates in the current directory a temporary file, the name of which begins with a tilde. When the document is correctly closed, the temporary file is deleted.

- If your system crashes and you lose a document, you can try opening the temporary file. The location of your temporary file is determined in the Options window.

1 Click **File**, **Open** to display the Open dialog box.

OR

On the Standard toolbar, click the **Open** button .

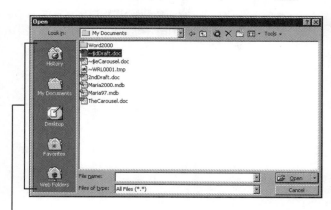

2 Click a folder button to change the file group displayed in the window:

- **History** —most recently accessed documents.

- **My Documents** —the folder where your files are saved by default.

- **Desktop** —an overview of your computer.

- **Favorites** —favorite folders and files that you have previously chosen.

- **Web Folders** —favorite folders collected from the World Wide Web.

18

3 Choose the desired folder:

    a. Click the **Up One Level** button 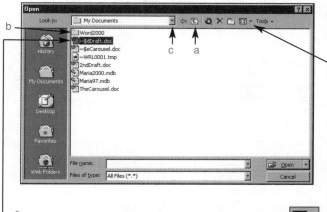 to display the folders that are stored along with the folder currently displayed in the **Look in** text box.

    b. Double-click a folder icon in the list window to display the contents of that folder.

    c. Click the **Look in** drop-down arrow to choose another disk drive.

4 Click the drop-down arrow next to the **Views** button to change the way the folder and file list is displayed:

- Choose **List** to show as many files as possible.
- Choose **Details** to show file information, such as size, type, and date modified.
- Choose **Properties** to show more file information about the currently selected file.
- Choose **Preview** to display a thumbnail image of the file.
- Choose **Arrange Icons** to change the order of the list.

5 Click the name of the file you want to open.

6 Click the **Open** button.

New Document

Create a new, blank file to create, edit, format, and print documents.

- When Word is first started, a new document based on the Normal template automatically appears on the screen.

- New documents can be blank documents based on the Normal template, or they can be based on pre-formatted templates for memos, letters, facsimiles, or other purposes.

Toolbar

1 Click the **New Blank Document** button 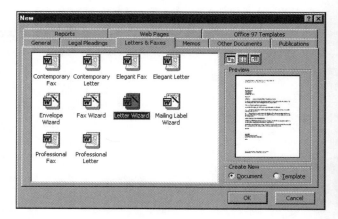.

2 A new, unnamed document based on the Normal template appears in the window.

Dialog Box

1 Click **File**, **New** to display the New dialog box.

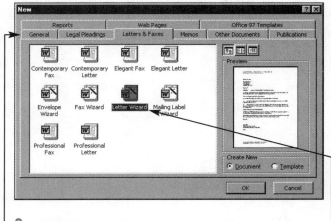

2 Click the tab for the type of new document you want to create.

3 Click the desired template icon for a new document. A preview of the template appears in the **Preview** area.

4 Click **OK** [OK].

Undo

This feature allows you to "undo" any mistakes you make in your document.

Notes:

- The keyboard shortcut to undo a task is **Ctrl + Z**; the shortcut to redo is **Ctrl + Y**.

- When you undo an action using the drop-down list, you undo all the actions above it on the list.

- Undo does not affect material cut or copied to the clipboard.

1 When you realize you've made a mistake, click the **Undo** button.

OR

To undo more than one step, click the **Undo** drop-down arrow, then click the desired number of steps to undo.

OR

Click **Edit**, **Undo**.

2 To redo a step, click the **Redo** button.

OR

To redo more than one step, click the **Redo** drop-down arrow, then click the number of steps to redo.

OR

Click **Edit**, **Redo**.

Continue →

Move Around in the Document

Most documents are too big to be completely viewed in the Word window. Here's how to get around your document quickly.

Notes:

- Changing the text you view does not change the position of the insertion point. You need to point and click where you want to make a change in the document. See *Move Insertion Point.*

- Another way to navigate an especially large document is to use the Document Map feature.

- See *Zoom* to view more than one page of a document at the same time.

Use the scroll bars to move where you desire:

a. the end of the document
b. the beginning of the document
c. a specific part of the document—click and drag the box
d. the right side of the page
e. the left side of the page
f. the previous page
g. the next page
h. select browse object, then move to the next or previous object

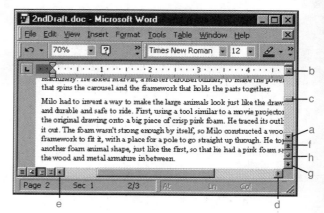

Click the **Select Browse Object** button and choose from the following:

→	Go to a particular page number
🔍	Find text
✎	Browse by Edits
≔	Browse by Heading
🖼	Browse by Graphic
▦	Browse by Table
{a}	Browse by Field

⬚	Browse by Endnote
⬚	Browse by Footnote
⬚	Browse by Comment
⬚	Browse by Section
⬚	Browse by Page

Scroll Using the Wheel on the IntelliMouse

An IntelliMouse has a wheel in the middle that can be used to scroll through documents.

Roll the wheel to scroll up and down in the document.

OR

1   Wheel-click the document window to change the vertical scroll bar.

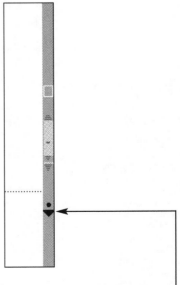

2   Point above or below the center divider to scroll up or down in the document. The farther you point from the center, the faster you scroll.

3   Wheel-click to go back to normal scrolling.

Move Insertion Point

The insertion point, usually appearing as a vertical line, can be placed on the page using the mouse or keystrokes.

Notes:

- You can't place the insertion point in margins or within the margin areas.

- To place the insertion point in a header or footer, double-click it.

Mouse

To move the insertion point, point to the desired location and click.

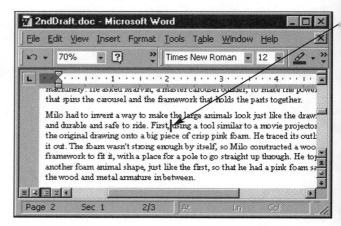

Keystrokes

Moves the insertion point:	Press:
One character left	Left arrow
One character right	Right arrow
One line up	Up arrow
One line down	Down arrow
One word left	Ctrl + Left arrow
One word right	Ctrl + Right arrow
One paragraph up	Ctrl + Up arrow
One paragraph down	Ctrl + Down arrow
End of the line	End
Beginning of the line	Home

Moves the insertion point:	Press:
Top of the window	Alt + Ctrl + Page Up
Bottom right of the window	Alt + Ctrl + Page Down
Up one screen	Page Up
Down one screen	Page Down
Top of next page	Ctrl + Page Down
Top of previous page	Ctrl + Page Up
End of document	Ctrl + End
Beginning of document	Ctrl + Home
Previous revision	Shift + F5
Location of insertion point when doc was last closed	Shift + F5

Tables

Moves the insertion point:	Press:
Next cell	Tab or Right arrow
Previous cell	Shift + Tab or Left arrow
Previous row	Up arrow
Next row	Down arrow
First cell in row	Alt + Home
Last cell in row	Alt + End
First cell in column	Alt + Page Up
Last cell in column	Alt + Page Down

Save

Until a document has been saved to a disk, any changes that have been made to it exist only in the computer's temporary RAM memory.

1 Click the **Save** button .

OR

Click **File**, **Save** to display the Save As dialog box.

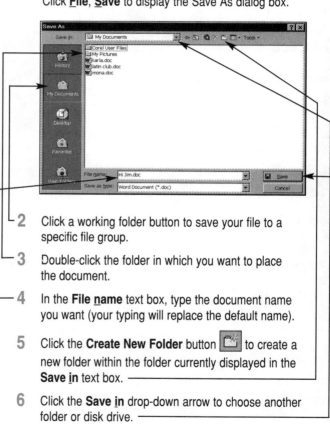

2 Click a working folder button to save your file to a specific file group.

3 Double-click the folder in which you want to place the document.

4 In the **File name** text box, type the document name you want (your typing will replace the default name).

5 Click the **Create New Folder** button to create a new folder within the folder currently displayed in the **Save in** text box.

6 Click the **Save in** drop-down arrow to choose another folder or disk drive.

7 Click the **Save** button.

28

Continue ⟹

Select Text

Selecting text, graphics, tables, and other information is one of the most basic actions in word processing. Many commands and features are designed to affect only selected information.

Notes:

• When text, graphics, or tables are selected, they appear surrounded by a block of color that will be different depending on your Windows settings. Information can be selected a number of different ways using the mouse and the keyboard.

Mouse

Select this:	By doing this:
A varying amount of text and graphics	Click and drag over information.
A single word	Double-click the word.
A single graphic	Click the graphic.
A line of text	Click in the left margin (the pointer becomes an arrow).
Several lines of text	Click and drag in the left margin (the pointer becomes an arrow).
A sentence	Press Ctrl, click the sentence.
A paragraph	Double-click in the left margin (the pointer becomes an arrow) or triple-click the paragraph.
Several paragraphs	Click and drag in the left margin (the pointer becomes an arrow).
A large amount of text and graphics	Click the beginning of the block, press and hold Shift and click the end of the block.
The entire document	Triple-click the left margin (the pointer becomes an arrow).
A vertical block of text	Press Alt, then click and drag over text.

Keyboard

Keyboard selections are relative to the current location of the insertion point.

Select this:	Press:
The character to the right	Shift + Right arrow
The character to the left	Shift + Left arrow
The rest of the word	Ctrl + Shift + Right arrow
The beginning of the word	Ctrl + Shift + Left arrow
The rest of the line	Shift + End
The beginning of the line	Shift + Home
One line down	Shift + Down arrow
One line up	Shift + Up arrow
The rest of the paragraph	Ctrl + Shift + Down arrow
The beginning of the paragraph	Ctrl + Shift + Up arrow
One screen down	Shift + Page Down
One screen up	Shift + Page Up
The beginning of the document	Ctrl + Shift + Home
The entire document	Ctrl + A
Specific blocks of text	F8 + arrow keys, then Esc to cancel

Select Text and Graphics in a Table

Select this:	Press:
The next cell	Tab
The preceding cell	Shift + Tab
Additional cells	Shift + desired arrow key
The column	Shift + Up arrow or Down arrow (repeat)
Additional columns or rows	Ctrl + Shift + F8, Esc to cancel
Fewer cells	Shift + F8
The entire table	Alt + 5 (numeric keypad only; Num Lock off)

Copy Information

Use the Copy command to copy text, formatting, and graphics and place them elsewhere in the document, or in a different document. Because it is such a common word processing task, there are several ways to copy information.

Drag-and-Drop Feature

1   Click and drag to select the text and graphics you want to copy.

2   Press and hold the **Ctrl** key, then click and drag the selected information to the new location (the insertion point will have a gray square and a square with a plus sign (+) inside it to indicate that you are dragging a copy).

3   Release the mouse button at the spot where you want the copied information to appear.

Toolbar

1   Click and drag to select the text and graphics you want to copy.

2   Click the **Copy** button.

3   Point to and click the spot where you want to paste the copied information.

4   Click the **Paste** button.

Menu

1   Click and drag to select the text and graphics you want to copy.

2   Click **Edit**, **Copy**.

3   Point to and click the spot where you want to paste the copied information.

4   Click **Edit**, **Paste**.

Cut/Move Information

Use the Cut and Paste commands to copy text, formatting, and graphics and place them elsewhere in the document, or into a different document. Because they are such common word processing tasks, there are several ways to cut and paste information.

Notes:

- The keyboard shortcut for cutting information is **Ctrl + X**.

- If drag-and-drop doesn't work, the Drag-and-Drop feature might not be turned on. To turn it on, click **Tools**, **Options**, and the **Edit** tab, then check **Drag-and-drop text editing** to select it.

- Cut information is placed on the Clipboard, where it remains until something new is copied or cut over it. (The Clipboard contents exist in RAM memory, and so are not saved when the system is shut down.)

- To cut and save more than one item, or to access other items saved to the clipboard, use the Paste All command.

- To copy information between applications, and still be able to edit the information in the source program, you can use the Embed or Link feature.

Drag-and-Drop

1 Click and drag to select the text and graphics you want to move.

2 Click and drag the selection to the new location (the insertion point will have a gray square to indicate that you are dragging information).

3 Release the mouse button at the spot where you want the information to appear.

Toolbar

1 Click and drag to select the text and graphics you want to move.

2 Click the **Cut** button.

3 Click the spot where you want to move the information.

4 Click the **Paste** button.

Menu

1 Click and drag to select the text and graphics you want to move.

2 Click **Edit**, **Cut**.

3 Click the spot where you want to move the information.

4 Click **Edit**, **Paste**.

Spelling

Word automatically checks the spelling of the words in your document and underlines with a wavy red line those it does not recognize.

Notes:

- The keyboard shortcut to start a spelling check is **F7**.

- The wavy red line under misspelled words does not print.

1 Right-click the misspelled word.

2 From the list of possible spelling choices, click the desired spelling.

OR

Click **Ignore All** to accept the word throughout the document.

OR

Click **Add** to permanently add the word to Word's dictionary.

Dialog box

1 Click **Tools**, **Spelling and Grammar** to open the Spelling and Grammar dialog box.

OR

Click the **Spelling and Grammar** button .

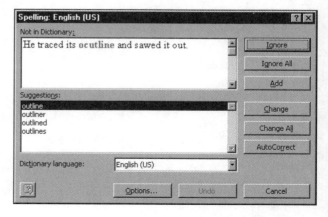

2 The first misspelled word will appear in the **Not in Dictionary** text box. You can do one of the following:

   a. Click the correctly spelled word in the **Suggestions** list and click the **Change** button [Change].

   b. Click the correctly spelled word in the **Suggestions** list and click the **Change All** button [Change All] to correct all identical misspellings throughout the document.

   c. Click the correctly spelled word in the **Suggestions** list and click the **AutoCorrect** button [AutoCorrect] to automatically correct the identical misspelling when you type it in the future.

   d. Click the **Ignore** button [Ignore] to leave the word as it is and go on to the next word.

   e. Click the **Ignore All** button [Ignore All] to ignore all instances of the word.

   f. Click the **Add** button [Add] to add the word to the dictionary for future spell checks.

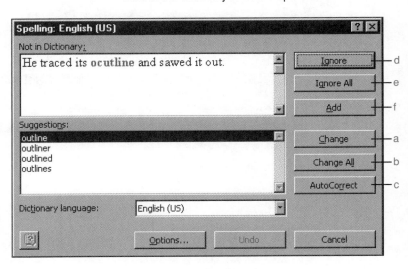

3 Repeat step 2 until all words are checked.

Align Text

Text can be aligned at the left or right margin, evenly justified between margins, or centered along a vertical axis.

Notes:

- To align text more than one way on a line, use Tabs (see *Tabs*).

- The keyboard shortcuts for aligning text are:

  Left: Ctrl + L

  Right: Ctrl + R

  Justified: Ctrl + J

  Centered: Ctrl + E

Toolbar

1 Click and drag over the text to be formatted.

  OR

  Point to and click the spot where you plan to type new text.

2 Click the desired toolbar button:

  - **Align Left** button.
  - **Align Right** button.
  - **Justify** (left and right align) button.
  - **Center** button.

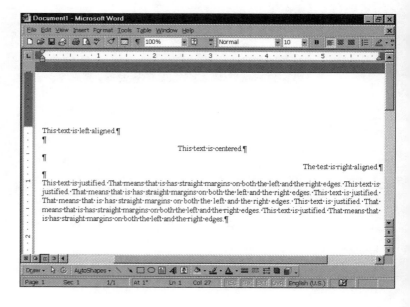

- To make lines closer to the same length (less ragged), change the hyphenation zone.

Dialog Box

1 Click and drag over the text to be formatted.

OR

Click the spot where you plan to type new text.

2 Click **Format**, **Paragraph** to display the Paragraph dialog box.

3 Click the **Indents and Spacing** tab.

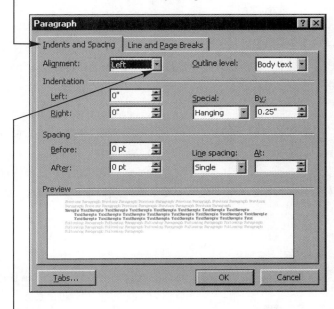

4 Click the **Alignment** drop-down arrow and click the desired alignment.

5 Click **OK**

Font

By formatting the font, you can change the typeface, appearance (such as bold or italic), size, color, and other aspects of the type in your documents.

Notes:

- Font attributes can be changed one at a time using the toolbar, or all can be accessed at once using the Font dialog box. The Font dialog box also contains additional attributes that are not available on the toolbar.

- The keyboard shortcuts to change fonts are:

  Bold:
  Ctrl + B

  Italics:
  Ctrl + I

  Underlined:
  Ctrl + U

  Larger:
  Ctrl + Shift + >

  Smaller:
  Ctrl + Shift + <

Toolbar

Click and drag over the text to be formatted.

OR

Point to and click the spot where you plan to type new text.

- To change the typeface, click the **Font** drop-down arrow
  `Times New Roman` and click the desired font.

- To change the font size, click the **Font Size** drop-down arrow
  `10` and click the desired size.

- To make the text bold, click the **Bold** button `B`.

- To italicize the text, click the **Italics** button `I`.

- To underline the text, click the **Underline** button `U`.

- To change the text color, click the **Font Color** drop-down arrow `A`.

- Click the **Text Effects** tab in the Font dialog box to animate fonts for e-mail or Web page design.

- Use WordArt to fill text with color effect or to change the shape of a word.

Using Font Dialog Box

1 Select the text to be formatted.

OR

Point to and click the spot where you plan to type new text.

2 Click **Format**, **Font** to display the Font dialog box.

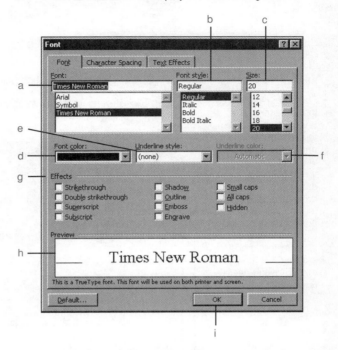

a. Scroll through the fonts in the **Font** list box and click the desired font (which fonts are listed will depend on which are installed on your computer).

b. Click a style in the **Font style** list box.

c. Click a size in the **Size** list box.

OR

Click the **Size** text box and type the desired point size.

d. Click the **Font color** drop-down arrow to choose the desired font color.

e. Click the **Underline style** drop-down arrow to select the desired underline style.

f. Click the **Underline color** drop-down arrow to choose the desired underline color.

g. Click an **Effects** check box to turn effects off or on.

h. View a preview of the formatted font in the **Preview** box.

i. Click **OK**.

Footnotes and Endnotes

Word automatically numbers and renumbers footnotes and endnotes when notes are added or deleted from the text.

1 Click to place the insertion point at the referenced text.

2 Click **Insert**, **Footnote** to open the Footnote and Endnote dialog box.

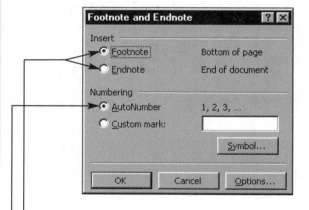

3 Click the option button for the desired type of note:
   - **Footnote** (appears at the bottom of the page)

   OR
   - **Endnote** (appears at the end of the document)

4 Click the **AutoNumber** option button to use normal Arabic numbering.

5 Click **OK**

6 The insertion point appears next to a superscript number at the bottom of the page or the document.

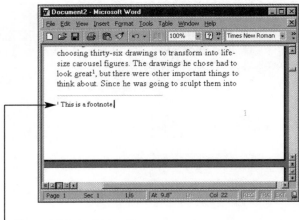

7 Type the desired note text.

View Footnote or Endnote Text

Point to the desired footnote or endnote number in the text. The note text will appear in a small window near the pointer.

Edit Footnote or Endnote Text

1 Point to the note number in the text and double-click to quickly find the note.

OR

Point to and click the note text.

2 Make the desired edits.

Delete a Footnote or Endnote

1 Click and drag over the superscript number in the body text of the document to select it.

2 Press **Delete**.

Move a Footnote or Endnote

1 Click and drag over the superscript number in the body text of the document to select it.

2 Click the **Cut** button ✂ or use any alternative cut, copy, or move command.

3 Click the desired new location in the body text.

4 Click the **Paste** button 📋 or use any alternative paste command.

Indent Paragraphs

Paragraphs can be quickly indented from the left using the toolbar buttons. Using the Paragraph dialog box, paragraphs can also be set with only the first line indented or with all lines following the first indented (a hanging indent).

Notes:

- Click the **Increase Indent** button repeatedly to move text farther to the right.

- A paragraph with a hanging indent has all lines after the first indented from the left.

Toolbar

1 Click and drag over the paragraphs to be indented.

OR

Point to and click the spot where you plan to type new paragraphs.

2 Click the **Increase Indent** button to move text to the right.

OR

Click the **Decrease Indent** button to move text to the left.

Change Indent Spacing

1 Click and drag over the paragraphs to be indented.

OR

Point to and click the spot where you plan to type new paragraphs.

2 If necessary, click **View**, **Ruler** to display the rulers.

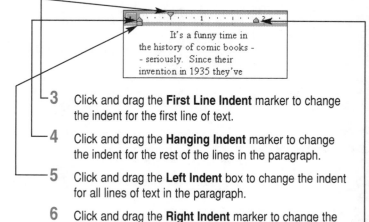

3 Click and drag the **First Line Indent** marker to change the indent for the first line of text.

4 Click and drag the **Hanging Indent** marker to change the indent for the rest of the lines in the paragraph.

5 Click and drag the **Left Indent** box to change the indent for all lines of text in the paragraph.

6 Click and drag the **Right Indent** marker to change the right indent.

- To set a hanging indent using the ruler, move the **Hanging Indent** marker to the right of the **First Line Indent** marker.

- Changes in indent settings affect only the current paragraph, unless more than one is selected.

Dialog Box

1 Click and drag over the paragraphs to be indented.

OR

Click the spot where you plan to type new paragraphs.

2 Click **Format, Paragraph** to display the Paragraph dialog box.

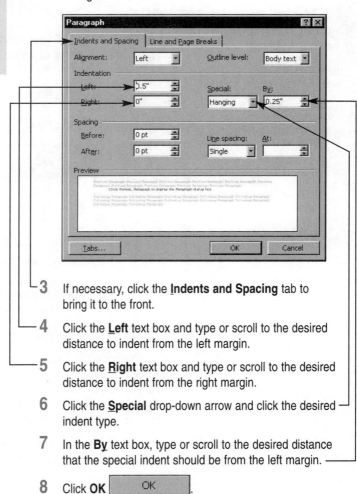

3 If necessary, click the **Indents and Spacing** tab to bring it to the front.

4 Click the **Left** text box and type or scroll to the desired distance to indent from the left margin.

5 Click the **Right** text box and type or scroll to the desired distance to indent from the right margin.

6 Click the **Special** drop-down arrow and click the desired indent type.

7 In the **By** text box, type or scroll to the desired distance that the special indent should be from the left margin.

8 Click **OK**.

43

Margin Settings

Page margins can quickly be changed using the ruler or they can be set to precise locations using the dialog box.

Notes:

- The vertical ruler is visible only in Print Layout view. The horizontal ruler is visible in all views.

- Word will warn you if the margins you set are smaller than your printer allows.

Ruler

1   If necessary, switch to **Print Layout** view 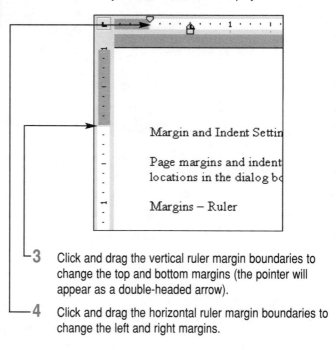 (the button is in the lower left corner of the document window).

OR

Switch to **Print Preview** .

2   If necessary, click **View**, **Ruler** to display the rulers.

Margin and Indent Settin

Page margins and indent locations in the dialog b

Margins – Ruler

3   Click and drag the vertical ruler margin boundaries to change the top and bottom margins (the pointer will appear as a double-headed arrow).

4   Click and drag the horizontal ruler margin boundaries to change the left and right margins.

Notes:

- With some specialized layouts (such as labels), you will get a warning that the page margins are too wide. Try ignoring the warning; sometimes the overage is blank area and to fix it would misalign the rest of the layout.

Dialog Box

1 Select the section of text where you want to change the margins.

2 Click **File**, **Page Setup** to open the Page Setup dialog box.

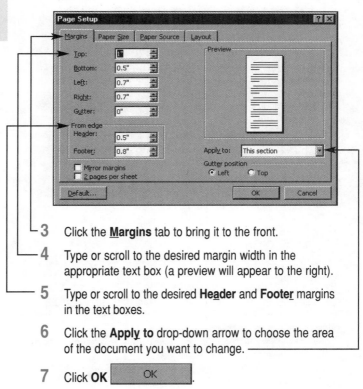

3 Click the **Margins** tab to bring it to the front.

4 Type or scroll to the desired margin width in the appropriate text box (a preview will appear to the right).

5 Type or scroll to the desired **Header** and **Footer** margins in the text boxes.

6 Click the **Apply to** drop-down arrow to choose the area of the document you want to change. ────

7 Click **OK**.

Page Break

Page breaks are used to begin a new page of text before the previous page is filled.

Notes:

- Word automatically inserts soft page breaks when the pages of a document are full of text and graphics. These breaks appear in Normal view as horizontal dotted lines. When information is added or deleted to the document, lines of text will slide over soft page breaks to keep the pages filled. A hard page break will end a page before it is filled with text and graphics. Text following a hard page break will always be at the top of the next page.

- The keyboard shortcut to insert a page break is **Ctrl + Enter**.

1 Click where the new page will start.

2 Click **Insert**, **Break** to display the Break dialog box.

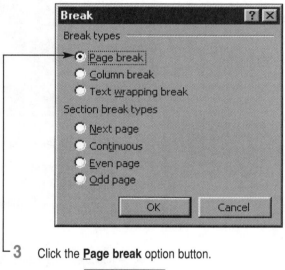

3 Click the **Page break** option button.

4 Click **OK** OK .

Continue ➡

Page Numbering

Use the Page Numbers feature to add page numbers to the top or bottom of your document pages.

Notes:

- For more elaborate page numbering, insert a page number field in the document header or footer, along with any other text you would like to include.

- Hide the page number on the first page by clearing the **Show number on first page** check box in the Page Numbers dialog box.

1 Click **Insert**, **Page Numbers** to display the Page Numbers dialog box.

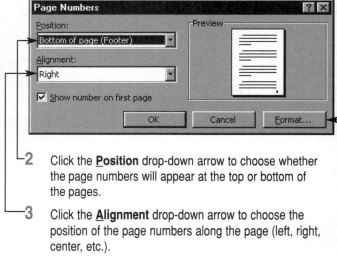

2 Click the **Position** drop-down arrow to choose whether the page numbers will appear at the top or bottom of the pages.

3 Click the **Alignment** drop-down arrow to choose the position of the page numbers along the page (left, right, center, etc.).

4 To change the default number format or to start page numbering at a number other than 1, click the **Format** button [Format...] to display the Page Number Format dialog box. ─────

* The number typed in the **Start at** text box will appear on the first document page of the section (unless the **Show number on first page** option is not selected).

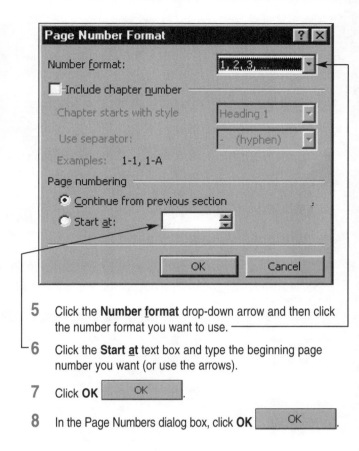

5   Click the **Number format** drop-down arrow and then click the number format you want to use. ────────

6   Click the **Start at** text box and type the beginning page number you want (or use the arrows).

7   Click **OK** [OK].

8   In the Page Numbers dialog box, click **OK** [OK].

Paragraph and Line Spacing

You can set different spacing between paragraphs and lines of text.

Format ➡ ≡¶ Paragraph...

1 Click where you intend to type text with new spacing.

OR

Click and drag to select already existing text.

2 Click **Format**, **Paragraph** to open the Paragraph dialog box.

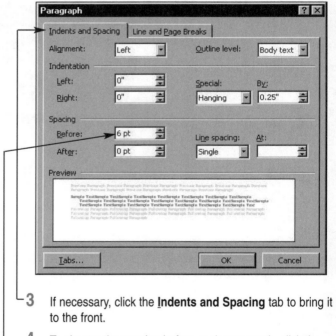

3 If necessary, click the **Indents and Spacing** tab to bring it to the front.

4 To change the spacing before each paragraph, click the **Before** text box and type the desired spacing (or use the arrows).

50

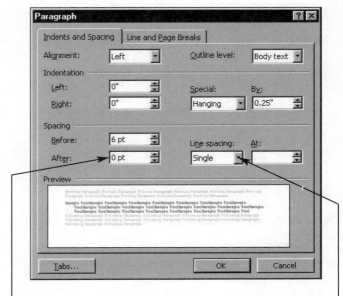

5 To change the spacing after each paragraph, click the **After** text box and type the desired spacing (or use the arrows).

6 To change the spacing between all lines, click the **Line spacing** drop-down arrow and choose the desired spacing:

   • **Single** for closely spaced lines
   • **1.5 lines** for half a line of space between each line of text
   • **Double** to alternate blank lines with text lines
   • **At least** to enter a minimum point distance in the **At** text box
   • **Exactly** to enter a point distance in the **At** text box
   • **Multiple** to add more than one blank line between each line of text

7 When finished, click **OK**.

Tabs

Use tabs to precisely left align, center align, right align, or decimal align text on the page.

Notes:

- Tab settings can be placed using the ruler or by selecting the additional options in the Tabs dialog box. (If the ruler is not visible, click **View**, **Ruler**.)

- Because word processor applications do not read space marking in the same way that typewriters do, it is best to use tabs to align text or objects on a page. You can also align text using a table (see *Tables*).

Ruler

1 Click and drag to select the text to be affected by tab settings.

OR

Click the spot where you plan to type and tab new text.

2 Point to and click the **Tab** button at the left edge of the ruler until the desired tab appears:

- **Left Tab** left aligns text on the tab.
- **Center Tab** centers text on the tab.
- **Right Tab** right aligns text on the tab.
- **Decimal Tab** aligns decimal points on the tab.

3 Click the desired location on the bottom edge of the ruler. A tab symbol will appear.

4 To move a tab, click and drag its symbol to a new location on the ruler.

5 To remove a tab, click and drag its symbol off the ruler.

Notes:

- Use different tabs for different alignments:

   Left Tab: text appears to the right of the tab.

   Right Tab: text appears to the left of the tab.

   Center Tab: text appears equally to the left and right of the tab.

   Decimal Tab: numbers appear to the left of the tab until a period is typed; numbers following the period appear to the right.

   Leader adds a line extending beyond the text to the edge of the page.

- To align text more than one way on a single line, use tabs.

- To create regularly spaced tabs, in the Tabs dialog box enter a distance in the **Default tab stops** text field.

- To insert a tab in a table, press **Ctrl + Tab**.

Dialog Box

1 Click and drag to select the text to be affected by tab settings.

   OR

   Click the spot where you plan to type and tab new text.

2 Click **Format**, **Tabs** to display the Tabs dialog box.

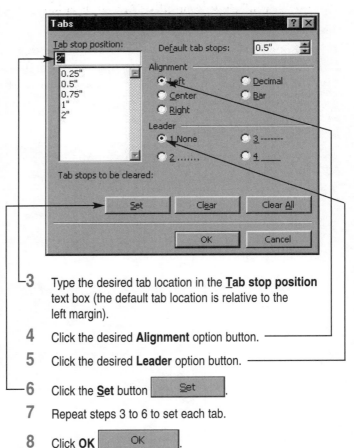

3 Type the desired tab location in the **Tab stop position** text box (the default tab location is relative to the left margin).

4 Click the desired **Alignment** option button.

5 Click the desired **Leader** option button.

6 Click the **Set** button.

7 Repeat steps 3 to 6 to set each tab.

8 Click **OK**.

Create a Table

Tables are useful for arranging text or numbers in columns or rows. Tables can be formatted with a variety of border and shading styles.

Notes:

- To create newspaper style columns, use the Columns feature.

Create a Simple Table

1 On the Standard toolbar, click the **Insert Table** button and drag over the desired number of columns and rows (you can also add and remove columns and rows later).

2 Click **Table**, **Table AutoFormat** to open the Table AutoFormat dialog box.

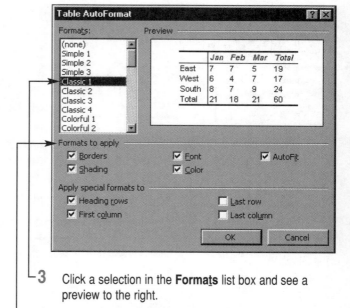

3 Click a selection in the **Formats** list box and see a preview to the right.

4 Click any **Formats to apply** check boxes to use or clear particular formatting.

5 Click **OK**.

6 To add information to the table, point to and click the first cell.

7 Type your information, then press **Tab** to move to the next cell.

Create a Complicated or Irregular Table

1   On the Standard toolbar, click the **Tables and Borders** button ⊞. The Tables and Borders toolbar appears, and the insertion point changes to a pencil shape.

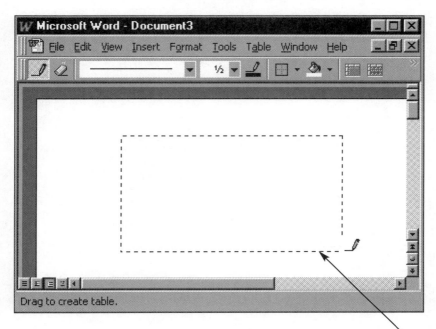

Drag to create table.

2   Click and drag to draw a rectangle the size of the desired table. ⎯⎯⎯⎯⎯⎯⎯⎯⎯⎯⎯⎯⎯

3   Click and drag to draw columns and rows inside the table.

4   To erase a line, click the **Eraser** button ✐ and drag over the line you want to remove. Click the **Eraser** button ✐ again to turn it off.

5   To add more lines, click the **Draw Table** button ✐ and click and drag. Click the **Draw Table** button ✐ again to turn it off.

6   To add information to the table, point to and click the first cell.

7   Type your information, then press **Tab** to move to the next cell.

Excel

Microsoft Office's spreadsheet application can be used to track and analyze numerical data for display on screen or in printed format. Excel is designed to help you record and calculate data, and present it in a clear and attractive manner. Excel provides you with various chart and layout options to enhance your spreadsheets. This book will help you to take full advantage of Excel's many abilities.

About the Excel Window

Excel provides an interface (graphical tools and controls) for working with worksheet data. This topic will help you identify the purpose of the tools and indicators that appear in the Excel window.

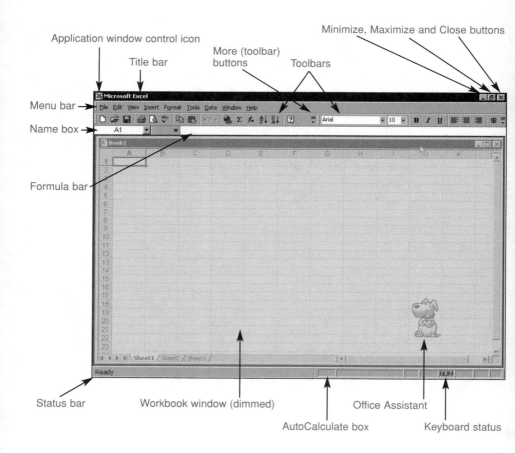

TIP: *You can set Windows to show more screen area, thereby showing more Excel workspace and toolbar buttons: Right-click the desktop, click* **Properties**, *click the* **Settings** *tab, then adjust the slider to select a resolution appropriate to your vision and monitor size. The screen area in the illustration above is set to 800 by 600 pixels.*

The Microsoft Excel Window

Application window control icon: Click to access a drop-down menu of commands that control the position and size of the application window.

Close, Maximize, and Minimize buttons: Click buttons to close, maximize, or minimize the Excel window.

Formula bar: Provides a space for typing or editing cell data.

Microsoft Excel title bar: Displays the program name (Microsoft Excel), and may also display the file name of an open workbook window, if the workbook is maximized. You can drag the title bar to move the window, or double-click it to maximize the window.

Menu bar: Displays menu names which, when clicked, display drop-down menus.

More buttons: Click to open a submenu of additional toolbar buttons. By default, Excel will add buttons that you use often to your toolbars, and remove buttons from the toolbar that you do not use.

Name box: Displays the cell reference of the active cell.

Office Assistant: Appears when you open Excel, and can answer your questions about how to perform a task.

Toolbars: Click toolbar buttons to select commands without opening a menu or dialog box.

Status bar: Displays information about the current mode, selected command, or option. The right side of the status bar shows the **keyboard status**. For example, NUM indicates that the numeric keyboard is toggled on (number lock). The middle of the status bar contains the **AutoCalculate box**, which displays the result of a selected AutoCalculate function (such as SUM or AVERAGE) when applied to a selected range of cells.

Workbook window: Appears in, and is restricted to, the Excel window. Workbook windows contain the data that you enter in worksheets (purposely muted in this illustration). You can open multiple workbook windows within Excel.

About Cells

Cells are areas in a worksheet in which you store data. In formulas, you refer to cells by specifying their column and row locations in the worksheet. This is called a cell reference. You can enter text, values, and formulas in cells.

Notes:

- Each cell is defined by the intersection of a row and a column (e.g., A3 denotes column A, row 3). The cell's location is called a **cell reference** (or cell address).

- When you open a new workbook, it usually contains multiple worksheets. Each worksheet has 256 columns and 65,536 rows. Therefore, each worksheet contains 16,777,216 cells!

- **Columns** are labeled A through IV. **Rows** are numbered 1 through 65,536.

- Each cell can store up to 32,000 characters.

- To select a cell, click it, or press an arrow key in the direction of the cell you want to select.

About Cell Locations

In the illustration below, cell B2 is the selected cell in Sheet1. You know this because:

- The reference B2 appears in the **name box**.
- Excel has outlined the column heading B and the row heading 2.
- Sheet1 is the active tab in the workbook window.
  NOTE: The contents of the selected cell also appear in the formula bar.

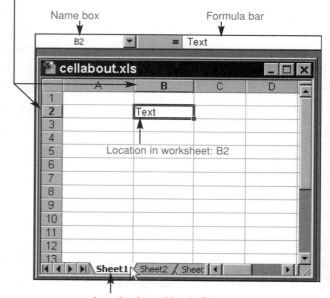

- A **control** is any graphical element that allows you to perform an action or specify a setting.

- Excel changes the shape of the mouse pointer when you rest it on a cell control, such as a cell border or fill handle.

- A **cell reference** indicates a cell's location. Cell references are often used in formulas to calculate values stored in the worksheet.

About Cell Properties and Controls

Cells are defined by the intersection of a column and a row. Therefore, the dimensions of a cell are defined by the column width and the row height. All cells have borders and fill properties. Selected cells have darkened borders and a fill handle (controls). These controls let you use a mouse to perform actions on the cell.

Border control: You can drag the border of a selected cell to move its contents.

Border style: You can apply line styles to one or more of the borders of a cell.

Fill: You can color or shade a cell to distinguish it from other cells.

Fill handle: You can drag the fill handle of selected cells to extend their content as a series, or, for a single cell, to copy its content to adjacent cells.

Height/width: You can change the column width and row height to adjust the size of a cell.

Location: You can identify the location of the selected cell by reading its cell reference in the name box (see illustration on previous page).

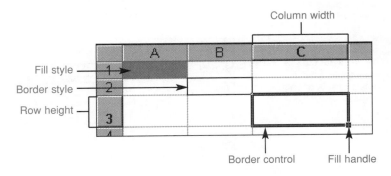

61

Select Cells, Columns, and Rows

When working with worksheets, you will need to select a cell or range of cells to complete a variety of tasks. A range may consist of adjacent or nonadjacent cells. You can also name and select named cell ranges. Keyboard shortcuts for selecting cells are listed in Help, on the Contents tab, under the "Keyboard Reference" topic.

Notes:

- Excel will scroll the worksheet when you drag the selection beyond the visible area of the worksheet.

- The first cell you select is the active cell (cell A10 in the illustration).

Select Adjacent Cell Range

1   Click first cell you want to select.

2   Drag mouse through cells to include in selection.

	A	B	C	D
9				
10	Date	Expense	Amount	Vendor
11	1/6/91	inventory	$16,000	SW Wholesale
12	3/5/91	inventory	$20,000	SW Wholesale
13	6/4/91	inventory	$16,000	SW Wholesale
14	8/5/91	inventory	$16,000	SW Wholesale
15	10/7/91	inventory	$14,900	SW Wholesale
16	12/5/91	inventory	$10,997	SW Wholesale

Notes:

- The first cell in the last range you select is the active cell (cell C10 in the illustration).

- Selecting nonadjacent cells or cell ranges (multiple selections) is often used to select data to chart.

Select Nonadjacent Cell Range

1   Click first cell and drag through cells to select.

2   Press and hold **Ctrl**. Then drag through additional ranges to include in your selection.

	A	B	C	D
9				
10	Date	Expense	Amount	Vendor
11	1/6/91	inventory	$16,000	SW Wholesale
12	3/5/91	inventory	$20,000	SW Wholesale
13	6/4/91	inventory	$16,000	SW Wholesale
14	8/5/91	inventory	$16,000	SW Wholesale
15	10/7/91	inventory	$14,900	SW Wholesale
16	12/5/91	inventory	$10,997	SW Wholesale
17	1/1/91	overhead	$1,000	A,B

Select Entire Column or Row

- Click row or column heading to select.

  TIP: You can click this Select All button to select the entire worksheet.

  Column heading

	A	B	C ✚	D
9				
10	Date	Expense	Amount	Vendor
11	1/6/91	inventory	$16,000	SW Wholesale
12	3/5/91	inventory	$20,000	SW Wholesale
13	6/4/91	inventory	$16,000	SW Wholesale
14	8/5/91	inventory	$16,000	SW Wholesale
15	10/7/91	inventory	$14,900	SW Wholesale

Row heading →

Notes:

- You can also name nonadjacent ranges, as shown on the previous page.

- You might want to name ranges that you frequently chart or print.

- You can also use the **Go To** command (**Ctrl + G**) to select named ranges.

Name a Range

1 Select the range to name.

2 Click in the **name box** and type descriptive name.

  NOTE: Range names may contain uppercase and lowercase letters, numbers, and most punctuation characters. They cannot include spaces. The underscore character is useful for simulating a space, as in "inventory_expenses."

3 Press **Enter**.

tory_expenses ▼		=	Date	
	A	B	C	D
9				
10	Date	Expense	Amount	Vendor
11	1/6/91	inventory	$16,000	SW Wholesale
12	3/5/91	inventory	$20,000	SW Wholesale
13	6/4/91	inventory	$16,000	SW Wholesale
14	8/5/91	inventory	$16,000	SW Wholesale
15	10/7/91	inventory	$14,900	SW Wholesale
16	12/5/91	inventory	$10,997	SW Wholesale
17	1/1/91	overhead	$1,000	A.B

Select a Named Range

- Click in **name box**, then click name to select.

Amount ▼		=	16000	
Amount		B	C	D
Database				
Inventory_expenses	Expense		Amount	Vendor
Vendors		nventory	$16,000	SW Wholesale
12	3/5/91	inventory	$20,000	SW Wholesale
13	6/4/91	inventory	$16,000	SW Wholesale
14	8/5/91	inventory	$16,000	SW Wholesale

Adjust and Hide Columns

Data appears in cells defined, in part, by the column width. You can control the width of columns or hide them. You can also adjust columns while print previewing your workbook.

Format ➡ Column

Notes:

- In step 2, the pointer's shape indicates when you can perform the action. It must be a cross with left- and right-facing arrows, as shown in the illustration.

- Column width is measured by the number of characters of the standard font.

Change Column Width Using the Mouse

To set width of multiple columns:

1   Drag through column headings of columns to change.

    OR

    Press **Ctrl** and click each column heading to change.

2   Rest pointer on right border of any selected column heading.

    Pointer becomes a **⟷**.

3   Drag pointer left or right to decrease or increase the column size. If you have selected nonadjacent column headings, press **Ctrl** while dragging pointer to uniformly change all selected columns. Excel displays width in a pop-up box as you drag.

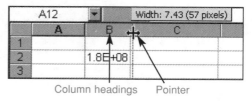

Column headings   Pointer

Notes:

- In step 1, you can select multiple columns.

Automatically Size Column to Fit Largest Entry

1   Rest pointer on right border of column heading. Pointer becomes a cross with arrows facing left and right.

2   Double-click.

BEFORE DOUBLE-CLICK   **AFTER**

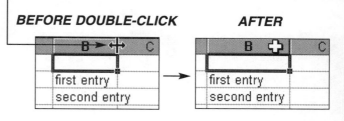

Notes:

- In step 1, you can drag through column headings to hide multiple columns.

- You can hide columns to prevent others from seeing the data, or to temporarily display columns of data next to each other for charting or other purposes.

Hide Columns by Dragging

1 Click column heading, then rest pointer on right border of selected column heading. Pointer becomes a ✛.

2 Drag pointer left beyond its own left border to hide the column.

BEFORE

C	D ✛	E
data1		data2
2	1111	2
3	1111	3
4	1111	4

AFTER

C ✛	E
data1	data2
2	2
3	3
4	4

Notes:

- In step 1, when the pointer is a cross with double vertical line and left- and right-facing arrows, you can perform the action.

Display Hidden Columns by Dragging

1 Rest pointer just to the right of column heading border. Pointer becomes a ✛|✛.

2 Drag pointer right to display the hidden column.

BEFORE

C ✛|✛	E
data1	data2
2	2
3	3
4	4

AFTER

C	D ✛	E
data1		data2
2	1111	2
3	1111	3
4	1111	4

Notes:

- Use the menu commands when you find it difficult to adjust columns with the mouse.

- In step 1, when using the menu to unhide columns, select the columns to the left and right of the hidden columns.

Adjust Columns Using the Menu

1 Select column(s) to adjust.

2 Click **Format**, **Column**.

3 Click desired column command.

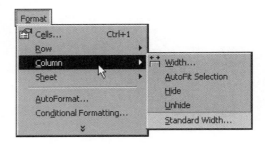

Align Data in Cells

Align cell data horizontally and vertically; apply text controls (wrap text in cells, shrink text to fit, merge cells); orient text in a variety of angles.

Notes:

- In step 2, if the desired alignment button is not visible, click the **More Buttons** arrow ⟩⟩ on the right side of the toolbar to view additional buttons.

- If no alignment is set, Excel applies the **General alignment** which left-aligns text and right-aligns values.

Align Cell Data Using Toolbar

1 Select cell(s) to align.

   NOTE: To select cells that are nonadjacent, you can press Ctrl and click or drag through cells.

2 Click desired alignment button on the Formatting toolbar:

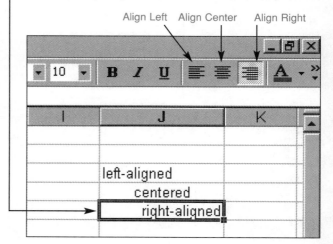

- In step 1, if **Merge and Center** button is not visible, click the **More Buttons** arrow ⟩⟩ to view additional buttons.

- A merged cell is one or more consecutive cells combined into one cell address.

- When you merge cells, only the contents of the upper-left cell are retained. That cell becomes the cell reference.

Merge and Center

1   Select cell containing data and drag to extend selection to include cells in which data will be centered.

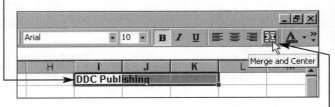

2   Click the **Merge and Center** button [🔲] on the Formatting toolbar.

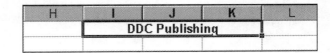

- Alignment options:

  Horizontal and **Vertical:** sets alignment of text in cells.

  Wrap text: inserts line breaks when needed and increases row height to fit text.

  Shrink to fit: shrinks characters to fit the column width.

  Merge cells: joins selected cells. The contents of the upper-left cell are retained. That cell becomes the cell reference.

  Indent: offsets data from left side of cell. Increments are measured in widths of characters.

  Orientation: sets the rotation of text. Increments are measured in degrees.

Menu Alignment Options

Set alignment options from a dialog box.

1   Select cells.

2   Click **Format**, **Cells**.

3   Click the **Alignment** tab.

4   Select desired options and click **OK** [OK].

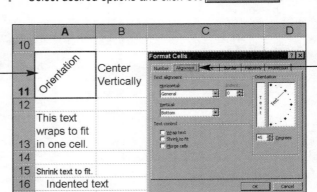

Clear Cell Contents

Using menu commands, you can clear either cell formats, contents, or comments, or clear all of these items.

Notes:

- In step 1, Excel will perform the clear command on all selected cells in one step.

- After you clear cells, you can the click **Edit** menu, then **Undo** to reverse the operation.

- Notice that after the **Clear Contents** command has been applied, the surrounding cells do not change position.

- When you clear a cell, the format of the cell, such as bolding or alignment, is retained.

Clear Cell Contents

Removes the contents (data and formulas) and leaves the cells blank in the worksheet without removing formats or comments.

1   Select cells to clear.

> NOTE: *To select cells that are nonadjacent, you can press* ***Ctrl*** *and click or drag through cells to include in the selection.*

2   Press **Delete**.

   OR

   - Right-click any selected cell.
   - Click **Clear Contents**.

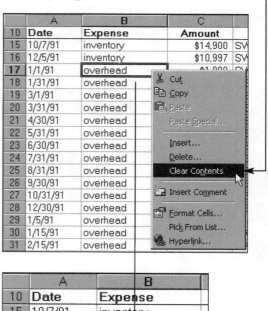

Cleared cell

Clear Cell Options Using Menu

Clears cell formats, contents, comments, or all of these items.

1 Select cells to clear.

NOTE: To select cells that are nonadjacent, you can press Ctrl and click or drag through cells to include in the selection.

2 Click **Edit**, **Clear**.

3 Click one of the following:

All   to clear formats, contents, and comments.

Formats   to clear only formats, such as border styles and font attributes.

Contents   to clear just the contents of the cell.

Comments   to clear just the comment attached to the cell.

Excel clears the cells as directed by your command.

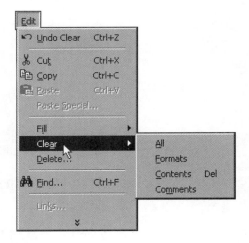

TIP: You can also clear cell contents by dragging the fill handle in a selection over the selected cells.

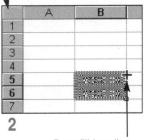

1

Pointer changes to a cross when resting on a fill handle.

Drag fill handle up.

2

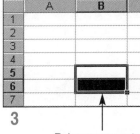

3

Release mouse to clear the cells.

Copy Cell Contents

You can copy data from one cell to another cell in a variety of ways. The method you choose often depends upon the location of the source and the destination.

Notes:

- Using menu commands to copy cells is must useful when both the source and destination cells are *not* in the same viewing area.

- In step 2, the flashing dashed outline remains until you press **Esc**, press **Enter**, or add input to another cell. The flashing outline indicates you can repeat the paste operation.

- In step 2 and step 4, you can also right-click the selected cells to access the **Copy** and **Paste** commands from a shortcut menu.

- **Caution:** When you paste data, existing data in the destination cells will be replaced. Click **Edit** menu, then **Undo** to reverse the paste operation.

- In step 4, to avoid overwriting data, click **Insert** menu, then click **Copied Cells**. The Insert Paste dialog box appears from which you can choose a direction to shift the existing cells.

Copy Cell Data Using Menu Commands

1 Select cells to copy. ————————————

2 Click **Edit**, **Copy**. A flashing dashed outline appears around cells.

3 Select destination cell. ————————————

4 Click **Edit**, **Paste**.

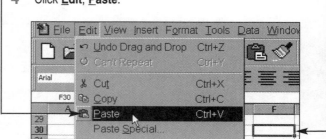

5 Repeat steps 3 and 4 to repeat paste operation.

6 Press **Esc** to end the paste procedure.

   *TIP: If you intend to paste the data only once, you can bypass steps 4-6 and just press **Enter**.*

Copy Cell Contents by Dragging Cell Border

1 Select cell(s) to copy.

2 Point to any border of selected cell(s).

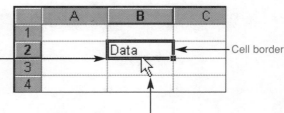

Cell border

Pointer becomes an arrow.

3 Press **Ctrl** and drag border outline to new location.

4 Release mouse button.

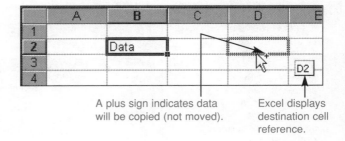

A plus sign indicates data will be copied (not moved).

Excel displays destination cell reference.

Copy Cell Contents by Dragging Fill Handle

1 Select cell(s) to copy, then point to fill handle. A crosshair appears.

Crosshair appears when pointer rests on fill handle.

2 Drag crosshair to extend border over adjacent cells to fill.

3 Release mouse button. Excel copies data into all cells within extended border.

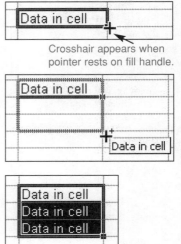

71

Delete Cells, Columns, or Rows

You can delete cells, rows, or entire columns, from a worksheet. Existing cells adjust to take the place of the removed cells.

Notes:

- In step 1, to select nonadjacent cells, you can press **Ctrl** and click or drag through cells to include in the selection.

- If deleted cells are used in formulas, the formulas will display #REF! error messages. If there are references to adjusted cells in formulas, Excel adjusts the formulas, even absolute references.

- **Caution:** You can lose data with the delete action. However, you can click **Edit** menu, then **Undo** to reverse the action.

- Do not confuse Delete with Clear. Clearing cells removes only the data, while deleting cells removes the cells from the worksheet.

1 Select cells to delete.

2 Click **Edit**, **Delete**.

If the Delete dialog box appears:

- Select the direction you want existing cells to shift.
- Click **OK** [OK].

	A	B	C	D
10	Date	Expense	Amount	Vendor
11	1/6/91	inventory	$16,000	SW Wholesale
12	3/5/91	inventory	$20,000	SW Wholesale
13	6/4/91	inventory	$16,000	SW Wholesale
14	8/5/91	inventory		holesale
15	10/7/91	inventory		holesale
16	12/5/91	inventory		holesale
17	1/1/91	overhead		
18	1/31/91	overhead		roperties
19	3/1/91	overhead		roperties
20	3/31/91	overhead		roperties
21	4/30/91	overhead		roperties
22	5/31/91	overhead		roperties
23	6/30/91	overhead		roperties
24	7/31/91	overhead	$1,000	A.B. Properties

Delete dialog box:
Delete
- ○ Shift cells left
- ● Shift cells up
- ○ Entire row
- ○ Entire column

[OK] [Cancel]

*TIP: In step 2, you can also right-click any selected cell, then click **Delete** from the shortcut menu.*

	A	B	C
10	Date	Expense	Amount
11	1/6/91	inventory	$16,000
12	3/5/91	inventory	$20,000
13	6/4/91	Cut	$16,000
14	8/5/91	Copy	$16,000
15	10/7/91	Paste	$14,900
16	12/5/91	Paste Special...	$10,997
17	1/1/91		$1,000
18	1/31/91	Insert...	$1,000
19	3/1/91	Delete...	$1,000
20	3/31/91	Clear Contents	$1,000
21	4/30/91		$1,000
22	5/31/91	Insert Comment	$1,000
23	6/30/91	Format Cells...	$1,000

Delete Entire Column or Row

1 Click row or column heading to select.

2 Click **Edit**, **Delete**.

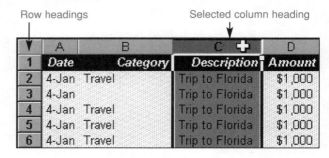

Row headings

Selected column heading

TIP: You can also delete cells by pressing **Shift** and dragging the fill handle in a selection over the selected cells.

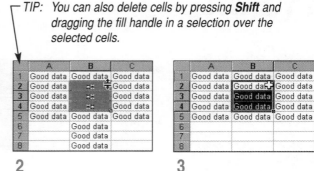

1

Pointer changes to a cross when you rest it on fill handle.

2

Drag fill handle up over cells while holding the Shift key.

3

Cells are deleted and cells shifts up in this example.

Edit Cell Data

A cell entry can be changed (edited) with a variety of techniques. When cell editing is enabled, the formula bar gains extra controls (buttons) and displays the cell contents both in the cell and in the formula bar.

Notes:

There are three ways to edit a cell entry:

- Double-click the cell.
- Click the cell, then click in the formula bar.
- Click the cell, then press **F2**.

When editing:

- Excel displays a flashing cursor where new input will be inserted.
- You can press the **Ins** key to toggle between insert and overwrite mode.
- The formula bar changes to include **Cancel**, **Enter** and **Edit Formula** buttons.
- When editing a cell, you can insert text stored from the Clipboard by pressing **Ctrl+V.**

Edit a Cell Entry by Double-Clicking

1   Double-click cell containing data to edit. ───────

Excel displays a flashing insertion pointer in the entry and extra controls next to the formula bar. ──┐

C2	▾ ✗ ✓ =	Cell entry	
	A	B	C	D
1				
2			Cell entry	
3				

Insertion pointer

2   Click in the entry to place the insertion pointer.

OR

Drag through characters to select (the next action will replace or delete your selection).

3   Edit the entry as needed:

- Type characters to insert.
- Press **Del** to delete characters to the right of insertion pointer or to delete the selection.
- Press **Backspace** to delete character to the left of the insertion pointer or to delete the selection.

4   Press **Enter**.

OR

Click the **Enter** button ✓ on formula bar.

Notes:

- Replacing cell data by typing over it is best when little or none of the original cell data will be retained.

Replace a Cell Entry

1 Select cell containing data to replace.

2 Type new data.

3 Press **Enter**.

OR

Click the **Enter** button 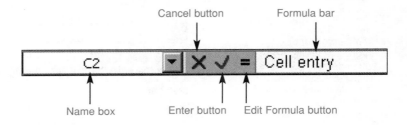 on formula bar.

Notes:

- Use **Esc** to undo your changes prior to completing it.

- If you have already entered the change, you can click the **Edit** menu, then **Undo**.

Cancel Changes to a Cell Entry

Prior to entering the change:

- Press **Esc**.

OR

Click the **Cancel** button ☒ on formula bar.

Notes:

- By default, Excel lets you edit cell contents directly in the cell. To set this option, click **Tools** menu, then **Options**; select the **Edit** tab; then select **Edit directly in cell**.

Formula Bar and Related Controls

Name box	Displays cell reference of the data you are editing.
Cancel button ☒	Lets you cancel a revision before completing it.
Enter button ✓	Lets you complete the revision.
Edit Formula button =	Provides help when editing formulas.
Formula bar	Lets you edit the cell content.

Cancel button   Formula bar

```
        C2        ▼  X ✓ =  Cell entry
```

Name box   Enter button   Edit Formula button

Enter Cell Data

Entering data is very straightforward. There are, however, many techniques for entering data of different types, such as dates, times, fractions, percents, and formulas.

Notes:

- In step 2, to wrap text within the cell, press **Alt+Enter**.

- In step 2, if what you type matches a previous entry in the current column, Excel's Auto-Complete feature fills in the text of the previous entry as you type.

- In step 3, you can also press an **arrow key** in the direction of the next cell you want to select, or click any other cell.

- In step 3, if what you enter matches an abbreviation in the AutoCorrect feature, Excel replaces the abbreviation with the specified replacement text.

- If no alignment is chosen, Excel applies the **General alignment** which automatically left-aligns text and right-aligns values (including dates and times).

- If your entry does not fit in the column, it overlaps into the next column, unless the next column cell also contains data.

Enter Text or Whole Numbers

1   Select cell to receive entry.

2   Type the text or whole number. A flashing insertion pointer appears after the data you type. The formula bar also displays your entry.

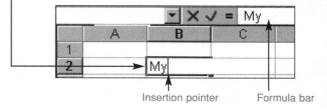

Insertion pointer   Formula bar

3   Press **Enter**.

OR

Click the **Enter** button ✓ on formula bar.

Excel completes the entry and selects the cell below it.

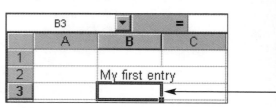

To cancel the entry before completing it:

- Press **Esc**.

OR

Click the **Cancel** button ✕ on formula bar.

*TIP: To enter identical data in multiple cells, select cells, type data, then press **Ctrl+Enter**.*

Enter Special Kinds of Data

1   Select cell to receive entry.

2   Type the data as shown in the table below. A flashing insertion pointer appears after the data you type. The formula bar also displays your entry.

3   Press **Enter**.

Category:	Example of what to type:
Currency	$25,000.25
Date	6/24/97
	24-Jun
	24-Jun-97
	Jun-97
Date and time	6/24/97 10 AM
Fraction	0 1/2
Label	text
Mixed number	1 1/2
Number	25
Number as label	="25"
Percent	25%
Time	10 AM
Formula (simple)	=A1+B1

*TIP: To enter today's date, press **Ctrl + ;** (semicolon).*

How AutoComplete Works

The AutoComplete feature assists you when entering repeating text in a column.

1   Select cell to receive text.

2   Type beginning of text. Excel automatically completes the entry (see highlighted text in illustration below) based on data previously entered in the column.

Categories
vegetable
stone
vegetable

NOTE: Type over the highlighted text to change it.

3   Press **Enter**.

Format Numbers

When you enter a value, Excel applies the format it thinks appropriate to your entry. You can also apply common number formats from the Formatting toolbar, such as Currency and Percentage; or you can select specific number formats using menu commands and the Format Cells dialog box.

Notes:

- In step 2, if the desired number format button is not visible, click the **More Buttons** arrow [>>] on the right side of the toolbar to view additional buttons.

- When you change a number format, Excel does not change the value.

- If the number does not fit in the cell after you change the number format, Excel displays ####### (pound signs) in the cell. To fix this problem, increase the column width, or select the **Shrink to fit** option.

- You can format a number when you enter it by typing specific symbols, such as a $ or %.

Format Numbers Using Toolbar

1 Select cell(s) containing values to format.

*NOTE: To select cells that are nonadjacent, press **Ctrl** and click or drag through cells to include.*

2 Click desired number format button on the Formatting toolbar:

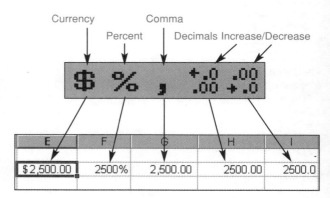

Format Numbers Using Menu Commands

1 Select cell(s) containing values to format.

   *NOTE: To select cells that are nonadjacent, **Ctrl** and click or drag through cells to include.*

2 Click **Format**, **Cells**.

3 Click the **Number** tab.

4 Select category of number format in **Category** list.
   Excel displays options for the selected category.

5 Select options for the category you have selected.
   Excel displays sample in **Sample** box.

6 Click **OK** OK when done.

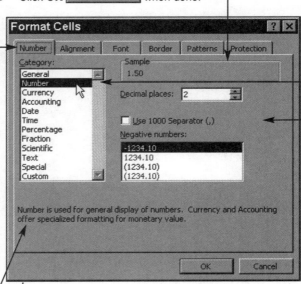

Category	Value	Comment
General	1.5	
Number	1.50	
Currency	$1.50	
Accounting	$ 1.50	
Date	January 1, 1900	*first day of century*
Time	1/1/00 12:00 PM	*first day and a half of century*
Percentage	150.00%	*you can set decimal places*
Fraction	1 1/2	
Scientific	1.50E+00	
Text	1.5	
Special	00002	*zip code*
	(718) 980-0999	*phone number*
	000-00-0002	*social security number*
Custom	1/1/1900 12:00 PM	*customized date and time*

Move Cell Contents

You can move data from one cell to other cells in a variety of ways. The best method to choose depends upon the location of the source data and its destination.

Notes:

- Using menu commands to move cells is best when the source and destination cells are *not* in the same viewing area.

- In step 2 and step 4, you can also right-click the selection to select the **Cut** and **Paste** commands from a shortcut menu.

- **Caution:** When you paste data, existing data in the destination cells will be replaced. Click the **Edit** menu, then **Undo** to reverse the paste operation.

- In step 4, to avoid overwriting data, you can click the **Insert** menu, then **Cut Cells**. The Insert Paste dialog box will appear, from which you can choose the direction to shift the existing cells.

- You may have to click the button at the bottom of the menu to view the **Cut Cells** command.

Move Cell Contents Using Menu Commands

1 Select cell(s) to move. ─────────────

2 Click **Edit**, **Cut**. A flashing dashed outline appears around selected cell(s).

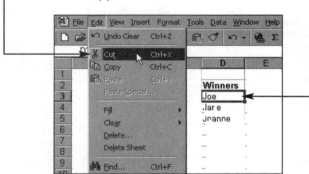

3 Select destination cell(s). ─────────────

4 Click the **Edit** menu, then click **Paste**.

OR

Press **Enter**.

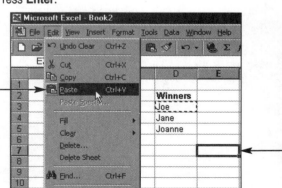

80

Move Cell Contents by Dragging Cell Border

1 Select cell(s) containing data to move.

2 Point to any border of selected cell(s).

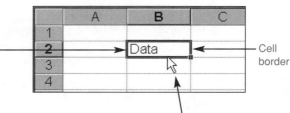

Cell border

Pointer becomes a solid arrow.

3 Drag border outline to new location.

4 Release mouse button.

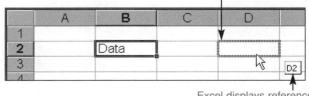

Excel displays reference of destination cell.

Move Part of a Cell's Contents into Another Cell

1 Double-click cell containing data to move. A flashing insertion pointer appears.

2 Drag through data to select it.

Excel highlights data in cell.

3 Press **Ctrl+X** (Cut).

4 Double-click destination cell and click where data will be inserted.

OR

Select cell to be overwritten by data.

5 Press **Ctrl+V** (Paste).

81

Sheet Tabs

Sheet tabs let you work with multiple worksheets within a single workbook file. You can select, group, insert, rename, delete, move, and copy sheet tabs.

Notes:

- In step 2, you can also press **Shift** and click to select consecutive sheets.

  Grouped sheets appear highlighted (white), while ungrouped sheets appear grey. When sheets are grouped, "[Group]" appears after the workbook name on the title bar.

- You can also ungroup sheets by clicking any sheet tab that is not currently grouped.

Group and Ungroup Sheet Tabs

When you group sheets, data and formatting changes made to the active sheet are repeated in the grouped sheets.

1 Click first sheet tab in group.

2 Press **Ctrl** and click each sheet tab to add to group.

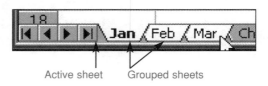

Active sheet   Grouped sheets

3 Click any grouped sheet tab to make it active.

To ungroup sheet tabs:

- Right-click any grouped sheet tab, then click **Ungroup Sheets** on the shortcut menu.

Notes:

- **Caution:** Be careful when deleting worksheets, because you cannot undo this action.

Delete Sheet Tabs

1 Right-click sheet tab to delete, then click **Delete** on the shortcut menu.

2 Click **OK** [OK] to confirm the action.

Insert...
Delete
Rename
Move or Copy...
Select All Sheets

View Code

82

Insert a New Sheet

1 Right-click any sheet tab, then click **Insert** on the shortcut menu. The Insert dialog box appears.

2 Click **Worksheet** icon, then click **OK** [OK].

3 Move and rename sheet tab as desired.

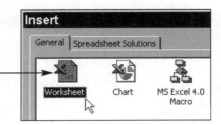

Rename a Sheet

1 Double-click sheet tab to rename. Excel highlights the sheet tab name.

2 Type new name, then click anywhere in worksheet.

Move and Copy Sheets

1 Select sheet(s) to move or copy. Excel highlights sheet tab names.

2 To move sheets, drag selection to desired location.

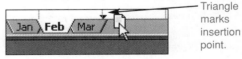

Triangle marks insertion point.

OR

To copy sheets, press **Ctrl** and drag selection to desired location.

Plus sign indicates copy.

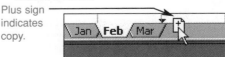

About Formulas

You will use formulas to calculate values stored in your worksheet. This topic explains basic information about formulas—formula location, formula parts, controlling the order of operation, and formula examples.

Formula Location

Enter a formula in the cell where the result should appear. As you type the formula, it will appear in the cell and in the formula bar. After you enter a formula, the result is displayed in the cell, and the formula is displayed in the formula bar.

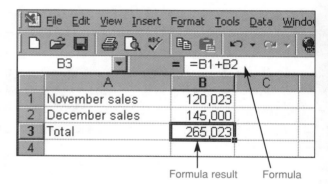

Formula result   Formula

Formula Parts

Formulas always begin with an equal sign (=) and often contain elements such as those shown in bold type in the following sample formulas:

numbers	=A1+**25**
cell references	=**A1**-25
reference names	=A1***Salary**
functions	=**Sum(A1:A10)**+Salary
operators	=A1/2+25*22-3
parentheses	=**(**24+A1**)**/2%

- When a formula contains both a multiplication and division operator, Excel performs the operations from left to right.

- When a formula contains both an addition and subtraction operator, Excel performs the operations from left to right.

Notes:

- Some of the examples contain named ranges. You must name a range before you can refer to it in a formula. However, Excel will let you use names when labels exist next to numbers in your worksheet.

Control the Order of Operations in Formulas

It is important to consider the order of mathematical operations when preparing formulas. Excel will perform the operation in your formulas in the following order:

- operations enclosed in parentheses ( )
- percentage %
- exponential ^
- multiplication and division * /
- addition and subtraction + -
- concatenation   (connection of text strings) &
- comparisons = < > <= >= <>

Formula Examples

This is a list of common formulas with a brief explanations:

=A1+25—adds the contents of cell A1 to the constant 25.

=A1-25—subtracts 25 from the content of cell A1.

=A1*TotalSalary—multiplies the content of cell A1 by the content of the cell named TotalSalary.

=Sum(A1:A10)+TotalSalary—adds the content of the cell named TotalSalary to the sum of cells A1 through A10.

=A10+(25*TotalSalary)—multiplies the content of the cell named TotalSalary by 25, then adds that result to the content of cell A10.

=A10^3—multiplies the content of A10 by itself 3 times (exponentially).

=2%*A10—two percent of the content of cell A10.

=(Min(Salary)+Max(Salary))/2—adds the minimum value in the range of cells named Salary to the maximum value in that range, and divides the result by 2.

=A10 & " " & A11—combines the text in cells A10 and A11 with a space between them. If A10 contains HELLO and A11 contains THERE, the result would be HELLO THERE.

=IF(A1<>0,A1*B10," ")—if the value in cell A1 is not zero, multiplies A1 by the value in B10, otherwise displays blank text.

Create Formulas (Simple)

Enter and build formulas to calculate values stored in your worksheet. This section includes basic information about building formulas, pasting names into a formula, and inserting references in formulas.

Notes:

- In step 1, select a cell in which you want to enter the result of the calculation.

- In step 2, when you type the equal sign, controls appear on the formula bar.

- In the illustration, the simple formula =25*A1 multiplies the value in A1 by 25.

- You can insert references until all the cells you want to calculate are included in the formula.

- If you decide to cancel the entry, press **Esc**.

Build Formula (Add References)

1 Select cell to receive formula.

2 Type an equal sign (=). The equal sign displays in the cell and in the formula bar.

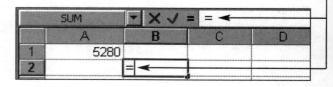

3 Type the formula.

To insert a reference in formula by pointing with the mouse:

- Click cell to reference. A dashed line appears around the cell, and Excel inserts the cell reference in your formula.

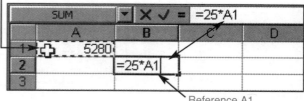

Reference A1

4 Type next part of formula. If formula is complete, go to step 5, below. Excel removes dashed outline, and your entry appears in cell and formula bar.

5 Press **Enter**.

OR

Click the **Enter** button ✓ on formula bar.

Excel calculates the formula and displays the result in the cell.

Notes:

- In step 2, you can also type the name of a range, instead of pasting it.

Paste a Named Range into a Formula

1 Place insertion point in formula.

2 Click **Insert**, **Name**.

3 Click **Paste** on the submenu.

4 Click name to paste in formula, then click **OK**

| OK |

Paste Name

Paste name
COM RATE
SALES

OK
Cancel

Notes:

- This procedure explains the steps needed to build a typical formula. References to the illustration appear in parentheses.

- When creating a formula, each time you point to a cell, Excel inserts it in the formula and outlines the cell.

- In step 4, each time you press **F4**, Excel changes the reference type.

- **Illustration result:** Formula in C7 should display 1360.

Create Formula, Insert Cell References, and Change Reference Type

1 Type the data in a new worksheet, as shown in the illustration below. Then create the formula in C7 to calculate the commission (=B2*C5).

	A	B	C	D
1		SALES COMMISSION		
2	COM RATE	4.00%		
3				
4		ELMHURST	CADDY	WUILLS
5	SALES	640000	340000	540000
6	BONUS	2000	1000	2000
7	COMMISSION	25600		
8	TOTAL COMP	27600		

2 Select cell to receive formula (C7).

3 Type = to start the formula.

4 Click cell for reference in formula (B2).

To change the inserted reference to absolute:

- Press **F4**. Reference changes to absolute (B2 becomes B2).

5 Type desired operator (*) .

6 Click next cell for reference in formula (C5).

7 Press **Enter** to complete the formula.

87

Create Functions

Functions are predefined formulas that perform specific calculations, such as finding an average or future value. Functions require arguments—the data to be calculated. To make it easy to create a function, Excel provides the Paste Function Wizard.

Paste Function button

Functions list on formula bar

Notes:

- In step 2, you can also click the **Insert** menu, then click **Function**.

- You can also click the **Paste Function** button when you want to insert a function in a formula you have already started to create.

- When creating a formula, you can click the **Function list** on the formula bar to insert frequently used functions and access the **Paste Function Wizard**.

- The **Paste Function Wizard** may insert a a suggested range in a **Number** box. Delete this range if it is not appropriate.

- As you click in a **Number** box, the Paste Function Wizard may add more boxes.

Insert a Function Using Function Wizard

1 Select cell in which to create the function.

2 Click the **Paste Function** button on Standard toolbar. The Paste Function dialog box appears.

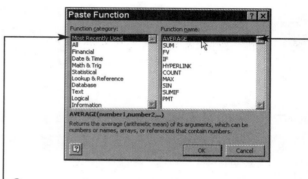

3 Select desired category in **Function category** list.

4 Select desired function in **Function name** list, then click **OK**. A dialog box for the function you selected appears.

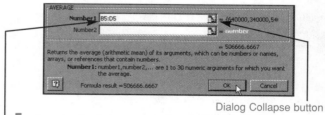

Dialog Collapse button

5 Insert cell references or values in **Number** boxes.

NOTE: You can click the **Collapse Dialog** button on the right side of the **Number** box, then select cells directly from the worksheet.

6 Click **OK** | OK | when done.

Edit a Function

1 Select cell containing the function to edit.
  NOTE: Do not double-click the cell.

2 Click the **Paste Function** button 𝒇ₓ on Standard toolbar.

3 Change arguments in **Number** boxes, then click **OK**.

Combine (Nest) Functions

1 Double-click cell containing function(s).

2 Place insertion point where new function will appear, or select argument to replace with a function.

3 Click the **Paste Function** button 𝒇ₓ on Standard toolbar.

4 Select desired category in **Function category**.

5 Select desired function in **Function name** list, then click **OK** | OK |.

6 Insert cell references or values in **Number** boxes.

7 Click **OK** | OK | when done.

| =AVERAGE(B5:B9,SUM(B6:D6)) |

Use AutoSum Function

1 Click cell in which function will be entered.

2 Click the **AutoSum** button Σ on the Standard toolbar. Excel surrounds suggested cells to add with dashed outline.

3 To change the range, drag through desired cells.

4 Press **Enter** when done.

	A	B	C	D	E
4		ELMHURST	CADDY	TOTALS	
5	SALES	640000	340000	=SUM(B5:C5)	
6	BONUS	2000	1000		

89

Edit Formulas

You will sometimes need to change a formula—perhaps replace an operator, add a set of parentheses, or change the cell or range to which the formula refers.

Notes:

- After you double-click the cell, Excel displays the formula in the cell and on the formula bar.

- To insert a function, click desired location in formula, then click the **Functions** button to the right of the formula bar (it shows the last function selected). Follow the prompts to insert the function.

- In step 2, if you drag through characters, your next action, such as typing, will replace the selection.

- If the edited formula displays an incorrect result, click the **Edit** menu, then **Undo Typing** to undo your change.

Edit Formulas

1 Double-click the cell containing the formula to change. Excel displays a flashing insertion pointer in the formula. Cell references in the formula are colored. Cell outlines indicate locations of references in worksheet.

VLOOKUP	▼	X ✓ =	=+C2+C3+C4+C5+C6+C7	
	A	B	C	D	E
1			Sales		
2		1992	4000		
3		1993	300000		
4		1994	35000		
5		1995	39000		
6		1996	43000		
7		1997	35000		
8		1998	222000		
9					
10					
11		Total	=+C2+C3+C4+C5+C6+C7		

2 Click in the entry to position the insertion pointer.

OR

Drag through characters to select. `=+C2+C3+C4+C5+C6+C7`

3 Edit the entry as needed:

- Type characters to insert.
- Press **Del** to delete characters to the right of insertion pointer or to delete the selection.
- Press **Backspace** to delete characters to the left of the insertion pointer or to delete the selection.
- Follow steps described on the next page to change reference or extend a cell range.

4 Press **Enter** or click the **Enter** button ✓ on formula bar.

OR

To cancel the change:

Press **Esc**, or click the **Cancel** button ✗ on formula bar.

Notes:

- Excel assigns a different color to each border and reference to help you identify them.

Change Reference in Formula

1 Double-click the formula to edit. Excel outlines references in worksheet with colored borders.

2 Point to border of outlined reference in worksheet.

Pointer becomes an 🗘 when positioned on border.

3 Drag border to desired cell or range.

Action: Drag border to cell containing new value to calculate.

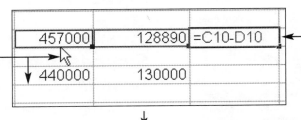

Result:

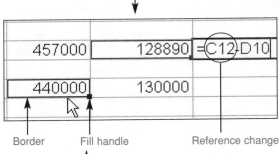

Border   Fill handle   Reference change

Notes:

- In step 2, the **fill handle** is a small square in the lower-right corner of the outlined reference.

Extend Cell Range in Formula

1 Double-click the formula to edit. Excel outlines references in worksheet with colored borders.

2 Point to fill handle of outlined reference in worksheet.

Pointer becomes a ➕ when positioned on fill handle.

3 Drag fill handle in direction to extend the range.

40000	20000
300000	15000
35000	33000
39000	25890
43000	35000

=SUM(C4:C8)

40000	20000
300000	15000
35000	33000
39000	25890
43000	35000

=SUM(C4:D8)   Reference change

In this example, range C4:C8 becomes...   C4:D8

91

Print Workbook Data

The Print feature lets you print the current worksheet, a selection in a worksheet, or an entire workbook. Additionally, you can specify which pages to print, collate printed pages, print multiple copies, and print to a file.

Print button

Settings that Affect Print Results

Before printing a worksheet or workbook, consider this checklist of settings that will affect print results:

Headers and footers: Prints repeating information at the top and bottom of each page.

Page breaks: Determines locations in worksheet where printed pages end and new pages begin.

Margins: Determines free space around printed page.

Orientation: Determines whether the page prints in portrait or landscape orientation.

Print area: Prints a specified area of the worksheet.

Repeating print titles: Prints column titles at the top or left side of each new printed page.

Scale: Determines the size of the worksheet information will be when printed.

Sheet options: Sets print options, such as gridlines, page order, draft quality, and black and white printing.

Print Using Toolbar

1 Select worksheets, worksheet cells, or chart object to print.

OR

Select any cell to print current worksheet.

2 Click the **Print** button ⊟ on the Standard toolbar.

Print Using Menu

1 Select worksheets, worksheet cells, or chart object to print.

   OR

   Select any cell to print current worksheet.

2 Click **File**, **Print**. The Print dialog box appears.

Change printer —

Click to preview —

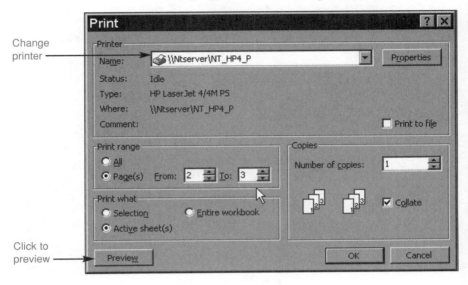

To indicate what to print:

• Select **Selection**, **Entire workbook**, or **Active sheet(s)**.

To specify pages to print:

• Select **All**, or select pages to print in **From** and **To** boxes.

To disable collating of printed pages:

• Deselect **Collate**.

To print multiple copies:

• Select number of copies in **Number of copies** box.

To print to a file:

• Select **Print to file**.

3 Click **OK** [OK] to print.

About Chart Items

While you create and modify charts, you will be presented with many choices and settings. Understanding the items in a chart and their properties will make it easier for you to design your own.

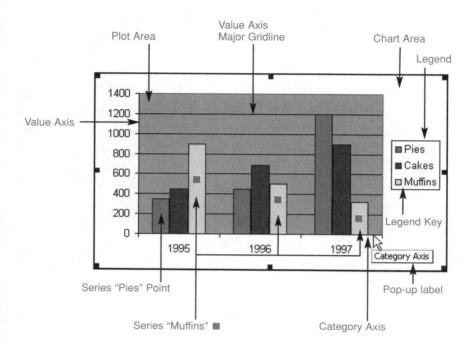

Notes:

- When you rest the pointer on any chart item, Excel displays a pop-up label identifying the name of the item.

Identify Chart Items

The default Clustered Column chart type shown above includes the following items. Item properties are also described.

Category Axis (X Axis)—the horizontal line on which categories of data are usually plotted. Properties include the format and alignment of category names and the scale of names and tick marks.

Chart Area—the space inside the chart. It includes the base properties of the chart, such as font style for chart text, background color, and how the chart moves or sizes when cells around it change.

Legend—a box containing a label and legend key for each series in the chart. Properties include its border, font, and placement.

- To review the properties of any chart item, rest the pointer on the item. When Excel displays the item name, double-click to display the Format dialog box for the item.

- Charts of different types have items or properties particular to their type. For example, pie charts have properties for a series that describe the angle of the first slice, while line charts have properties such as drop lines and up-down bars.

Legend Key—a graphic in the legend whose color or pattern corresponds to a series in the chart. Legend key properties include border, color, shadow, and fill effects.

Plot Area—the area within which the chart axes and series data is drawn. The properties include its border, area color, and fill effects.

Series—a group of data markers or series points that visually describe the values plotted. For example, the Series "Muffins" describes the number of muffins sold in each category (1995, 1996, and 1997). The properties of data series include borders and colors, plot axes, error bars, data labels, series order, and options such as overlap and gap width.

Series Point—a single item in a data series that visually describes the value for one category. For example, Series "Pies" Point indicates a value of 345 for the category 1995. The properties for series points include border and pattern, data labels, and options such as overlap and gap width.

Value Axis (Y Axis)—the vertical line that describes the values of series points in the chart. Properties include line and tick marks, scale of major and minor values, font for displayed values, number style of values, and text alignment.

Value Axis Major Gridlines—a set of lines that visually define values across the plot area. These gridlines help determine the value of a given series point in the chart. Properties include color, style, pattern, and units of values.

Create a Chart

Chart Wizard provides prompts and options for selecting the chart type, the source data, chart options, and chart location.

Chart Wizard button

Notes:

- Your selection will determine the orientation of the series in your chart. You can change this orientation in **Chart Wizard - Step 2 of 4** on the **Data Range** tab.

- Avoid blank rows and columns when selecting data to chart. Use the **Ctrl** key and drag through ranges to create a multiple selection and omit blank cells.

- You can hide rows and columns that do not pertain to data to be charted.

- In **Chart Wizard**, you can click **Next>** or **<Back** to move forwards or backwards to any step.

- **Chart Wizard - Step 1 of 4:** Select the chart type, then the subtype. Click and hold the **Press and hold to view sample** button to preview how the selected chart type will plot your chart.

Create a Chart

1 Select cells containing labels and values to chart.

   NOTE: You can change this selection as you proceed if you discover that you require different data.

2 Click **Chart Wizard** button on Standard toolbar.

   From Chart Wizard - Step 1 of 4 - Chart Type:

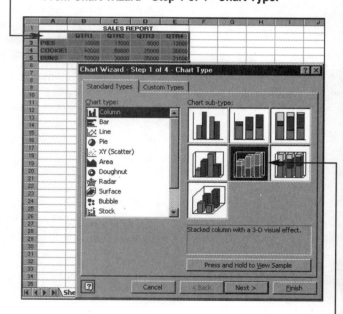

a. Select chart type and subtype (see *Select Chart Type*).

b. Click the **Next** button Next >.

From Chart Wizard - Step 2 of 4 - Chart Source Data:

• From the **Data
Range** tab, you can
change the range of
data to plot, or
change the
orientation of the
data series to
columns or rows.

• From the **Series** tab,
you can add and
remove series and
change references to
series names, data
ranges, and the
category (X) axis
labels.

**Chart Wizard -
Step 3 of 4:**

• From the **Chart
Options** dialog box,
you can set options
for chart titles, axes,
gridlines, legend,
data labels, and the
data table. You can
return to this dialog
box after the chart
is created.

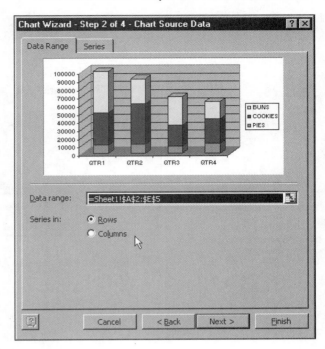

a. Select **Data Range** and **Series** options (see *Set Source
of Chart Data*).

b. Click the **Next** button Next >.

From Chart Wizard - Step 3 of 4 - Chart Options:

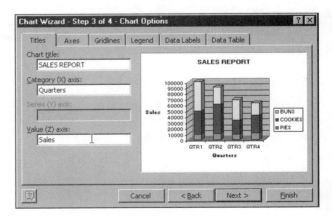

a. Select desired **Chart** options (see *Set Chart Options*).

b. Click the **Next** button Next >.

Create a Chart

(continued)

Notes:

Chart Wizard - Step 4 of 4:

- From the **Chart Location** dialog box, you can change the proposed destination sheet, or the proposed chart sheet name.

- You can click **Finish** from any **Chart Wizard** step to create the chart with default options.

From Chart Wizard - Step 4 of 4 - Chart Location:

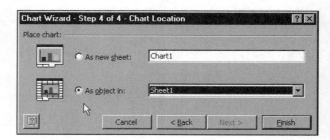

a. Select **As new sheet** or **As object in** (see *Set Location of Chart*).

b. Click the **Finish** button [**Finish**].

98

Access

Microsoft Office's database application is designed to create tables, forms, and reports based on records that you create. Access helps organize this information, and to use it as the basis of queries or searches, which filter the data in specified ways. Access helps you to manage large amounts of information and to show relationships among records. Like all other Microsoft Office applications, Access also allows you to arrange your data in visually attractive formats.

Display Objects in the Database Window

Each database has a Database window that displays the objects (such as forms, reports, tables, etc.) in the currently open database. You can customize how Access displays objects in the window.

Notes:

- The Database window is always open when you are working in a database. However, it might be minimized or hidden behind other open windows. Press **F11** to display it.

- Access menus are context-sensitive. This means that the options on menus vary depending on what you are working on. For example, the View menu contains one set of options when the Database window is active and another set when, for example, a table or Switchboard is open.

1 If the Database window is not on your screen, press **F11** or click the **Database Window** button 📇 to display it.

2 To change the icon size if desired:

- Click the **Small Icons** button ⬚.
- Click the **Large Icons** button ⬚.

NOTE: This changes the size of both the icons representing database objects and the buttons in the Database window.

3 To hide or show extra information about each database object if desired:

• To show only the object name, click the **List** button .

• To display additional information about each database object, click the **Details** button . The following illustration shows the Database window in Details view.

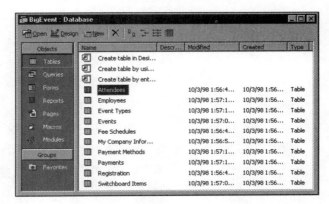

4 To arrange the database icons in a different order if desired:

a. Right-click the background of the window pane to open the shortcut menu.

b. Click **Arrange Icons**.

c. Select a sort order from the menu. For example, to sort objects alphabetically according to their names, you would click **By Name**.

Change the Default Database Folder

Specify the folder in which Access will save new databases that you create.

Tools ➡ Options...

1 Select **Tools**, **Options**. The Options dialog box displays.
   NOTE: You can do this only if a database is open.

2 Click the **General** tab.

3 Type the pathname of the default folder.

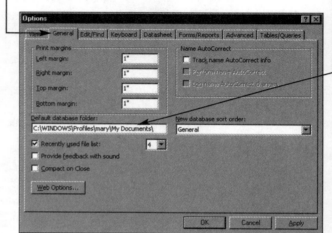

4 Click **OK**   OK   .

102

Continue ➡

Personalized Menus

The personalized menus feature places the commands you use most at the top of each menu and hides the commands that you do not use as often.

Notes:

- Access continually rearranges menu items by moving commands closer to the top of the menu and hiding commands that you do not use often. Because of this, when you open a menu, the command you are looking for might have been moved or hidden.

- When a menu contains hidden commands, an arrow symbol appears at the bottom of the menu. To unhide commands, click the arrow or pause the mouse pointer on the menu until the full menu is displayed.

- When menu commands are hidden, an arrow symbol appears at the bottom of the menu. Click the arrow to open the full menu.

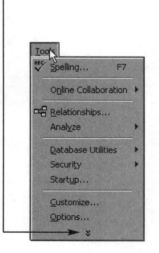

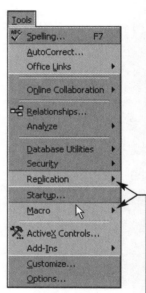

- When you open the menu, commands that were formerly hidden are shown using lighter shading.

104

Notes:

- If you want menu commands to remain where they are, disable personalized menus.

- You enable or disable personalized menus for each individual database.

Disable or Enable Personalized Menus

1 Select **Tools**, **Customize**. The Customize dialog box displays.

2 Click the **Options** tab.

3 To return all menus to their original state before commands were moved (does not remove menu customizations you have made yourself) if desired:
a. Click the **Reset my usage data** button

    Reset my usage data . A prompt displays.

b. Click the **Yes** button Yes .

4 To disable personalized menus, deselect **Menus show recently used commands first**.

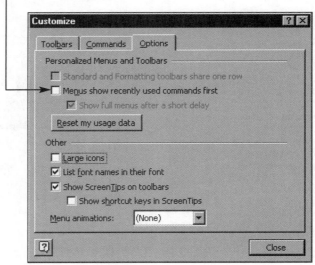

5 Click the **Close** button Close .

Create a Database Using a Wizard

A database contains tables, queries, forms, reports, and code modules. Office 2000 provides a number of database designs that you can use to create a database. Using the Database Wizard and database designs, you can quickly create a complete database.

Notes:

- The Database Wizard creates either a generic database or a database based on a design that you choose.

- When you use the Database Wizard to create a database based on a design, the wizard creates the database objects that you need. This includes tables, reports, forms, switchboards, and other database objects.

1   If you just launched Access, click **Access database wizards, pages, and projects** at the startup Microsoft Access dialog box and click **OK** OK .

OR

If the above dialog box is not on your screen, press **Ctrl+N**.

2   To create a database based on a design, click the **Databases** tab and double-click an icon.

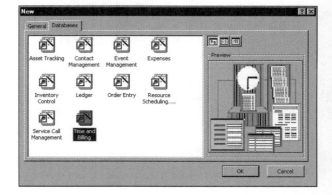

Notes:

• Not all available designs are installed when you install using Typical installation. If a particular design does not appear in your version of Access, run Setup to install it. See Access online Help for information on running Setup to add Access components.

OR

To create a database not based on a design, click the **General** tab and double-click the **Database** icon.

NOTE: If you use this option, you won't get the Database Wizard.

3 Select a folder in the **Save in** list or click a button representing a folder to specify the folder in which to save the database.

4 Type a file name for the database.

5 Click the **Create** button ![Create]. The Database Wizard starts and displays the first Database Wizard dialog box which describes the database.

6 Click the **Next** button ![Next >] to display the next dialog box. The contents of the Database Wizard screens vary depending on the database design that you chose in step 2. The remainder of this procedure shows you the dialog boxes for creating a database used for Time and Billing data.

7 Select fields to include in the database in the **Fields in the table** list. Clear the fields that you do not want to include.

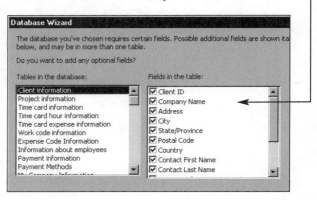

Create a Database Using a Wizard

(continued)

Notes:

- After you use the Database Wizard to create a database, you can modify the database objects in Design view to customize it.

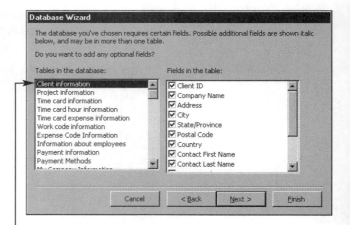

To view fields in another table, select a table in the **Tables in the database** list. The right pane shows fields in the selected table.

8 Click the **Next** button Next > .

9 Select a format for screen displays. A sample of the selected format displays in the preview pane.

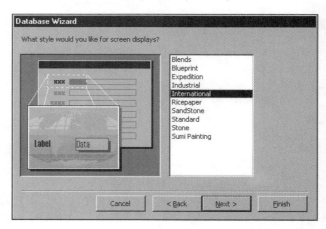

10 Click the **Next** button Next > .

- The Database Wizard dialog boxes vary depending on the database design that you choose. This procedure shows the dialog boxes for creating a database based on the Time and Billing design.

11 Select a report style.

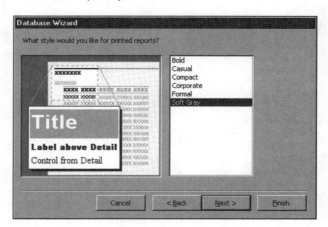

12 Click the **Next** button | Next > |.

13 Type a name for the database (does not have to be the same as the file name that you entered in step 4).

14 Click the **Next** button | Next > |.

15 To open the new database, click the **Finish** button

| Finish | at the last Database Wizard dialog box.

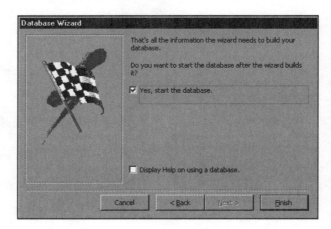

The Wizard creates the database.

Open a Database

Opens an existing database and displays the objects (such as tables, reports, forms, etc.) in the database in the Database window.

Notes:

- Only one database can be open at a time in Access.

- In Access 2000 you can search for a file from the Open dialog box. You do not need to use a separate utility to locate a file.

- By default, Access saves new databases in the My Documents folder.

If You Are Already in Access:

1 Press **Ctrl+O**. The Open dialog box displays.

2 To display the file to open if necessary:
- Click a button corresponding to the folder.
- Select a different folder from the **Look in** list.

- Click the **Views** button and select an option to display different information about files in the Open dialog box (for example, click the **Details** option to view information such as the file size).
- Click **Tools**, **Find** to search for a filename.

3 Double-click the file to open.

- How you open the database depends on whether you have just started Access, in which case the Startup dialog box is on the screen, or whether you are already working in the program.

- The Microsoft Access Startup dialog box appears each time you start Access unless you disable it.

If You Just Launched Access:

1 Select **Open an existing file** in the Microsoft Access startup dialog box.

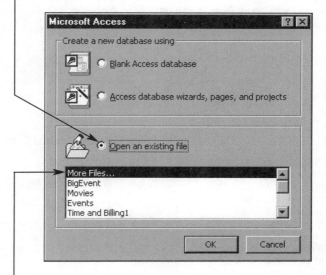

2 Double-click a database to open.

OR

Double-click **More Files** to display the Open dialog box. See step 2 on the previous page ("If you are already in Access") for a description of this dialog box.

Link to a Table in Another Access Database

Linking allows you to use the data located in a table in another Access database. For example, you could include the data from the external table in a report created in the current database. Note: a database must be open.

Notes:

- When you link a table, you do not have to recreate and maintain separate tables with identical data in two databases. For example, you might need to use information from an Employee table in both the Employee database and the Sales database.

- When tables are stored on a network server, you need to link them in order to access them.

- You can edit the data in the linked table either from the current database or from the database in which it was created.

- You cannot edit the underlying structure of a linked table. For example, you cannot add or delete a field from a linked table. You must open it in the original database to modify the structure.

1 Select **File**, **Get External Data**, **Link Tables**. The Link dialog box displays.

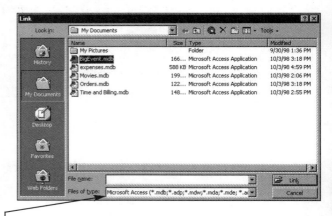

2 Select **Microsoft Access** in the **Files of type** list.

3 Select the database containing the table to link.

4 Click the **Link** button 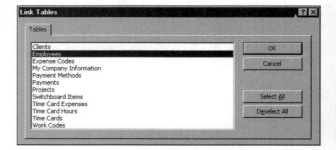. The Link Tables dialog box displays.

Notes:

- This arrow appears only in the database in which you created the link, not in the database in which the table was created.

5 Select the table to link and click **OK** [OK] .

6 In the Database window, the icon for a link to a table has an arrow next to it.

➤ ▪⊞ Customers

Notes:

- Removing the link does not delete the linked table. To access the table, open it in the database in which it was created.

Remove the Link to a Table

1 Open the database containing the link.

2 Select the link icon in the Database window.

3 Press **Delete**.

4 At the prompt, click **Yes**.

Create a Table Using a Wizard

Tables contain the data that you enter into a database. The Table Wizard walks you through each step of creating a table.

Notes:

- You can create a table using the Table Wizard and then open it in Design view to customize the table structure if necessary.

- Create a separate table for each type of information that will be stored in a database. For example, create one table to store product information and another to store information about companies that supply the products.

- One field in every table should identify each record in the table as unique. This field is called the primary key. Often this is an AutoNumber field, which automatically adds a sequential number to each record when it is created. You can also create a primary key from multiple fields if one field alone will not uniquely identify records.

1 Open or create a Database.

2 Press **F11** to display the Database window.

3 Click **Insert**, **Table**. The New Table dialog box displays.

4 Double-click **Table Wizard**. The Table Wizard starts.

5 Select one of the Sample Tables on which to model your table. The list of Sample Fields changes depending on the selected Sample Table.

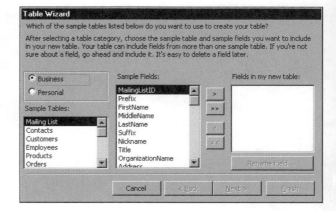

- These instructions assume that this table is the first added to a new database. If you are adding a table to a database that already has at least one table, an additional dialog box displays, allowing you to define relationships between the new and existing tables.

6 Select a field to add to your new table, then click $\boxed{>}$. Repeat until all fields that you want to include are listed in the **Fields in my new table** pane.

TIP: To add all of the fields in the Sample Fields list to the table, click $\boxed{>>}$.

7 To rename a field in your table if desired:

a. Click the field to rename.

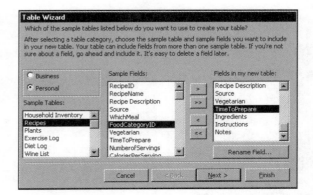

b. Click the **Rename Field** button $\boxed{\text{Rename Field...}}$.

c. Type the new field name and press **Enter**.

8 Click the **Next** button $\boxed{\text{Next >}}$.

9 Type a name for the table and click the **Next** button $\boxed{\text{Next >}}$.

10 The final step in the Table Wizard allows you to choose what happens next. Select an option and then click the **Finish** button $\boxed{\text{Finish}}$.

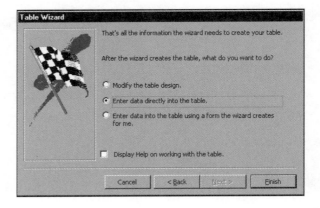

Add a Field to a Table

Modify the structure of a table by adding a new field.

Notes:

- When you add a new field to a table, the new field is not automatically added to forms and reports that you have created. If you want the field to appear in forms and reports, open the form or report in Design view and add the field.

- Use field properties customize fields.

1 Open the table in Design view (see **Open a Table**).

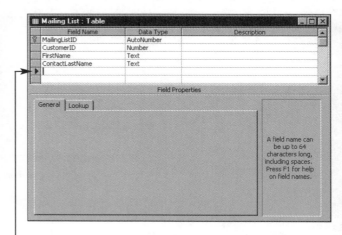

2 Click the first available blank row in the field list. An arrow appears next to the field.

OR

To insert a new field above an existing field, click the field that will be directly below the new field and select **Insert**, **Rows**.

3 Type a field name in the **Field Name** column.

4 Press the **Enter** or **Tab** key to move to the **Data Type** column.

5 Click 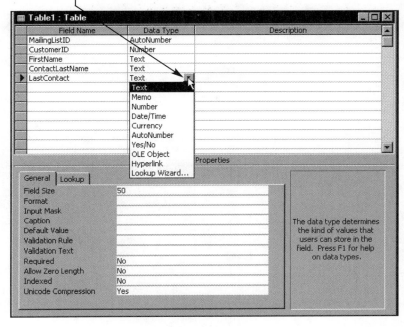 to open the list of data types (by default, new fields are Text type) and select the data type for the new field.

6 Press **Enter** or **Tab** to move to the **Description** column and type a description of the field if desired.
NOTE: The Description is optional. You can leave it blank.

7 Press **F6** to switch to the Field Properties pane.

8 Type the number of characters for the field in the **Field Size** property.

9 Set other properties if desired.

10 Click the **Save** button on the Database toolbar to save your changes.

11 Click the **Cancel** button to close the table design when you have finished modifying it.

Create a Simple Select Query

A simple select query returns a subset of the data in a table.

Notes:

- You can create a simple select query to show only a subset of the fields in a table. For example, you could create a query that shows only the company name and region and does not display the company address.

- A simple select query can also display a subset of the records in a table. For example, you could create a query that retrieves all contacts in a particular Zip Code.

1 Select **Queries** in the Database window.

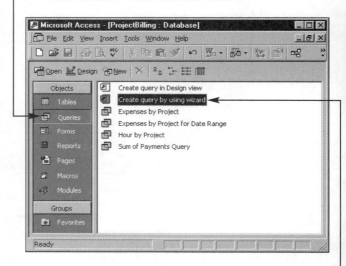

2 Double-click **Create query by using wizard**. The first Simple Query Wizard dialog box displays.

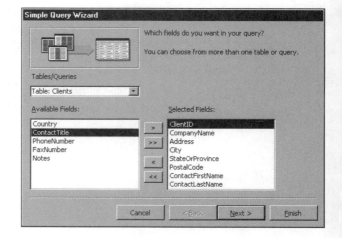

3 Select a data source for the query.

4 Select the fields to include in the result table.

5 Click the **Next** button | Next > |.

6 Follow the wizard dialog boxes. The dialog boxes that display depend on the data source that you choose.

7 Type a name for the query.

8 To enter criteria to select only records from the data source that meet the criteria, select **Modify the query design**.

9 Click the **Finish** button | Finish |. The query opens in Design view.

10 Type the criteria for the records to include in the result table in the Criteria row for the field. For help on entering criteria you can:
   • Press **Shift+F2** to open the zoom box to give you more room to type long expressions, or
   • Right-click in the Criteria field and select **Build** to start the Expression Builder.

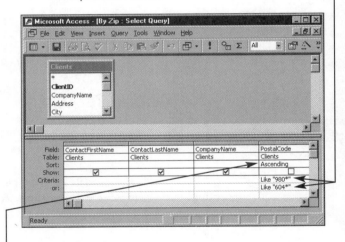

11 To sort the result table by a field, select **Ascending** or **Descending** in the Sort field to determine the sort order.

   For example, the above query retrieves clients located in a particular range of zip codes.

12 Click the **Save** button 🖫 on the Database toolbar to save the query design.

13 To run the query and view the results, select **View**, **Datasheet View**.

119

Enter Data in a Datasheet, Form, or Page

Use Datasheet view or Form view to edit the data in a table. These procedures also apply to data access pages that include data entry capabilities.

Open a Form or Datasheet for Data Entry

1 To open a datasheet, click **Tables** in the Database window.

OR

Click in the first blank field of the first blank row of the datasheet or form.

OR

To open a form, click **Forms** in the Database window.

2 Double-click on the form or datasheet name to open it.

Add a Record

1 Click the **New Record** button .

OR

If you enter data in the last record, a new record wil automatically appear at the end of the table.

2 Type data in the first field.

3 Press **Tab** to move to the next field.
   NOTE: You can also use arrow keys to move from field to field.

4 Repeat steps 2 and 3 to enter data in fields.

5 When finished adding records in the datasheet or form, click the **Cancel** button [X] to close it.

- When a field is long, you can open the current field in a zoom box to see all of the data in the field.

- If the font on the datasheet is small, you can relieve your eyes by using the Zoom box to edit fields. You can change the font size in the zoom box to a larger font.

Zoom to Enter Field Data

1 Position the cursor in the field you want to edit in the Zoom box.

2 Press **Shift+F2**. A Zoom box opens.

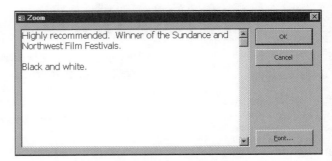

3 To view field contents in a smaller or larger font if desired:

    a. Click the **Font** button [Font...]. The Font dialog box displays.

    b. Select font and/or font size.

    c. Click **OK** [OK] to return to the Zoom box.

4 Type field data. To start a new paragraph, press **Ctrl+Enter**.

*NOTE: If you press **Enter** the Zoom box will close.*

5 To close the Zoom box, press **Enter**.

Copy Data from Previous Field

1 Click in a blank field below a filled-in field.

2 Press **Ctrl+ '** (apostrophe). Access copies the value from the same field in the previous record.

Enter Data in a Datasheet, Form, or Page *(continued)*

Undo Last Edit

Click [⤺] or press **Ctrl+Z** to undo the last edit in the current field. Repeat if desired to undo previous edits in the current field.

OR

Press **Esc** to undo all edits in the current field.

OR

Press **Edit**, **Undo Saved Record** to undo all edits to an entire record if you have already moved to another record but have not yet started editing it. If this command does not appear on the Edit menu, then you cannot undo changes to the record.

Delete Record

1   Position the cursor in the record you want to delete.

OR

Select the records you want to delete.

2   Click the **Delect Record** button [⋈]. Access displays a prompt to confirm that you want to delete the record(s).

3   Click the **Yes** button [Yes] to permanently delete the record(s).

4   Close the datasheet or form.

Navigate in a Datasheet, Form, or Page

Move around when editing table data.

Edit → Go To

Notes:

- Both forms and datasheets include navigation buttons (unless specifically removed in a form). Data access pages created for data entry purposes also include navigation buttons.

- Navigation buttons are located at the bottom of the window.

Use Navigation Buttons

1. Open a datasheet, form, or page for editing.

2. Click a record navigation button:

    |◄ | first record

    ◄ | previous record

    ► | next record

    ►| | last record

    ►＊ | new record

Go To a Record Number

1. Press **F5**.

2. Type the number of the record to go to.

Record: |◄ ◄   7 ► ►| ►＊ of 91

3. Press **Enter**.

Go to a Field by Selecting the Field Name (Datasheet View)

Notes:

- The Go To Field list shows all the fields in the datasheet. It is located on the Formatting toolbar, which is not displayed by default. If working in a datasheet with many fields, display the Formatting toolbar so that you can access this handy tool for navigating the datasheet.

1. Select **View**, **Toolbars**, **Formatting**.

2. Select the field to go to from the **Go To Field** list at the left of the Formatting toolbar: CompanyName ▼

123

Find Data in a Form or Datasheet

Find particular data in a field in a form or datasheet.

Notes:

You can use the following wildcard characters in both the Find and Replace dialog boxes:

* Matches any number of characters. Example: "*one" finds "fone" and "phone."

? Matches any single character. Example: "r?n?" finds "ran" and "run."

[ ] Matches any character in the brackets in the current position in the word. Example: "Hamm[oe]nd" finds "Hammond" or "Hammend"

[!] Matches any character not found in the brackets (excludes characters in brackets). Example: "Hamm[!oe]nd" will not find "Hammond" or "Hammend" but will find "Hammind"

[-] Matches a range of characters in ascending order. Example: "b[a-c]d" finds "bad" and "bbd" and "bcd"

Matches a single numeric character. Example: "980#0" finds 98010, 98020, etc.

1 Click the **Find** button ![binoculars icon] on the toolbar. The Find and Replace dialog box opens with the Find tab selected.

2 Type the text to find in the **Find What** text box.

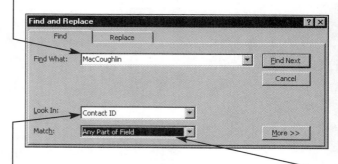

3 Select the field to search for the text.

4 Use the **Match** field to specify where the data can be located in the field in order for Access to find it.

5 To show additional options, click the **More** button

More >> .

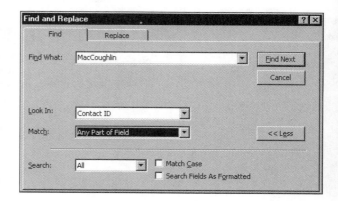

Notes:

- You can also use filters to find records meeting criteria. Filters hide any data not meeting your criteria.

- To find zero-length strings, type "" in the Find What box. Do not enter a space between the quotes. To find a null value, type **Null** or **Is Null** in the Find What box. You cannot use these in the Replace dialog box.

6   To specify which records to search, select a **Search** option:

   Up—From the current record to the first record.

   Down—From the current record to the final record.

   All—From the current record to the end of the database and continuing from the first record.

7   To find field data only when it is in upper/lowercase exactly as typed in the **Find What** box, select **Match Case**.

8   To find data only when it is formatted according to the data type of the text to find, select **Search Fields As Formatted**. For example, if you want to find the date 06-01 only in a formatted date field, select this option.

   NOTE: Selecting this option may slow down search performance.

9   To search for the next instance of the **Find What** text, click the **Find Next** button | Find Next |.

10 Repeat step 9 to find data as necessary.

11 Click the **Cancel** button | Cancel | or press **Esc** when finished.

Filter Records in a Datasheet or Form

Use filters to display a subset of the data in a table according to the criteria you specify.

Records ➡ Filter

Notes:

- Filters tell Access to hide data that you specify. For example, you can view only records for customers in a particular state or only movies with a certain actor in them.

- You can use Filter by Form in either Datasheet view or Form view. This procedure shows Datasheet view in the illustrations.

- If you enter criteria in an **Or** tab, the resulting filtered recordset will be those records that meet the criteria specified in either the **Look for** tab or the **Or** tab. The **Or** tab effectively broadens the scope of the filter. For example, you could show only records where the state is Washington *or* Missouri.

- To improve the speed of applying a filter, use indexed fields. If you often need to filter on a nonindexed field, consider indexing it.

Use Filter by Form

1   Select **Records, Filter, Filter by Form** in the datasheet or click the **Filter by Form** button [icon]. Access displays a datasheet with one blank row or a blank form. The tab at the bottom of the window is the **Look for** tab.

2   Click in a field to enter criteria.

3   Type the criteria to find.

    OR

    Click [▼] and select the data to find in the field.

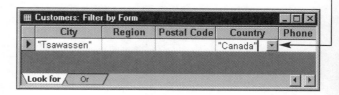

4   To add more criteria if desired, click the **Or** tab at the bottom of the window.

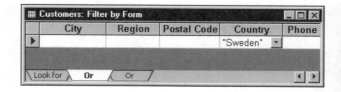

NOTE: *To clear all criteria from the filter if desired,*
*click the **Cancel** button* [X] *or select **Edit**,*
***Clear Grid**.*

5   Type or select criteria.

6   Repeat steps 4 and 5 to add more criteria if desired.

7 Click the **Apply Filter** button ▼. Access displays only records matching your criteria. The following illustration shows the records returned using the criteria shown in this procedure.

Use a Filter by Selection

1 Select the data to include in the filter. The filter will show only those records that have the selected data in them.

2 Select **Records, Filter, Filter by Selection** or click the

Filter by Selection button ⧀.

The filter hides all records that do not have the selected data in the field. The following illustration shows the results of the Filter by Selection set up in this procedure in Datasheet view.

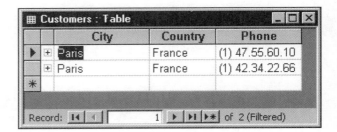

127

Filter Records in a Datasheet or Form

(continued)

Notes:

- The Filter Excluding Selection shows all records in the datasheet except for records that contain the data that you select. For example, if you select "Paris" in the City field, the filter hides all records except those with "Paris" in the City field.

Use a Filter Excluding Selection

1 Select the data to hide.

2 Select **Records, Filter, Filter Excluding Selection**.

Notes:

- Use this toolbar button to remove any type of filter. Records hidden by the filter are now shown.

Remove Filter and Show All Records

- Click the **Remove Filter** button .

Continue

Sort the Data in a Datasheet or Form

Perform a quick sort in Datasheet view or Form view if you only need to sort on one field. Or, use the Advanced Filter/Sort window to sort on multiple fields.

Records ➡ Filter

Notes:

- Sort in either ascending or descending order by one field only.

Sort on the Current Field

1 Open the table in Datasheet view or Form view.

2 Position the cursor in the field to sort on.

3 Click the **Sort Ascending** button to sort in ascending order.

OR

Click the **Sort Desceding** button to sort in descending order.

Notes:

- Data will be sorted on fields in the order that they appear in the grid (left to right) in the Advanced Filter/Sort window. For example, to sort by last name and then first name, you would first add the Last Name field to the grid. The sort order set up in the illustration is first by country, then region, then city.

Sort on Multiple Fields

1 Open the table in Datasheet view or Form view.

2 Select **Records**, **Filter**, **Advanced Filter/Sort**.

3 Drag a field to sort on from the field list to the grid.

OR

Click in the **Field** row and select the field to sort on.

4 Select a **Sort** order for the field.

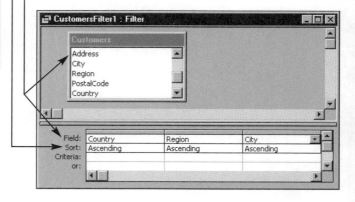

130

5   Repeat steps 3 and 4 for each field you want to sort on. The above illustration shows a sort order with three fields.

6   Set up the sort order as desired:

   • To reorder fields, you can move a field by clicking the column selector (above the field name) and then dragging it to a different position in the grid.

   • To insert a column after a field in the grid, position the cursor in the field and select **Insert**, **Columns**. The new column is inserted after the field containing the cursor.

   • To remove a field from the sort order, click the column selector for the field and press **Delete**.

   • To completely clear the design grid so that you can start over, select **Edit**, **Clear Grid**.

7   Select **Filter**, **Apply Filter/Sort**. Access sorts the data and returns to Datasheet view or Form view.

8   Click the **Remove Filter** button [icon] to remove the sort order if desired.

Create a Form Using a Wizard

Forms are usually used to provide a user interface for data entry.

Notes:

- A form displays the data in one or more data sources (tables or queries). When you create a form using the Form Wizard, you choose which fields from which tables or queries will appear on the form.

1 Click **Forms** in the Database window.

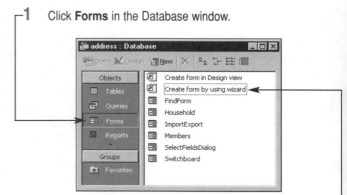

2 Double-click **Create form by using wizard**. The Form Wizard starts.

3 Select the record source for the form.

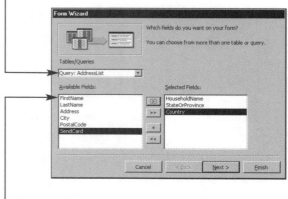

4 Select fields to include in the form in the **Available Fields** list and click [>].

NOTE: *To select multiple fields, press **Ctrl** and click the next field to select.*

OR

Click [>>] to include all of the available fields in the form.

5 Repeat steps 3 and 4 to add fields from other record sources to the form as desired.

6 Click the **Next** button Next > .

7 Select a layout for the form.

NOTE: Click on a form layout to see a sample of the layout in the preview pane. See also Create a Form using AutoForm *for examples of the Tabular and Columnar layout.*

8 Click the **Next** button Next > .

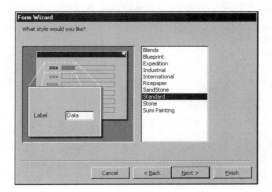

9 Select a style for the form.

10 Click the **Next** button Next > .

11 Type a name for the form.

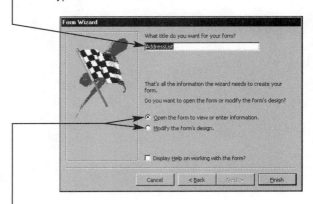

12 Specify what you want to do next: view the form, or open it in Design view for further customizing.

13 Click the **Finish** button Finish . The form appears.

Create a Multiple-Tab Form

Use tab controls to divide a form into multiple pages. Tab forms have a tab at the top, which you can click to move between them.

Notes:

- Use a multiple-tab form to organize fields into different pages.

- Multiple-tab forms are often used to create dialog boxes. If you use Microsoft software, this type of form is already familiar to you.

1 Select **Insert**, **Form**. The New Form dialog box displays.

2 Select **Design View**.

3 Select the data source (table or query) for the form.

4 Click **OK**. A blank form design window opens.

5 Click the **Tab Control** button on the Toolbox. The mouse pointer changes shape as shown in the illustration below.

NOTE: *If the Toolbox is not displayed, select View, Toolbox.*

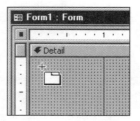

6 Drag across the form grid to create a form of the desired size. When you release the mouse button, a tab control with two tabs is added to the design grid.

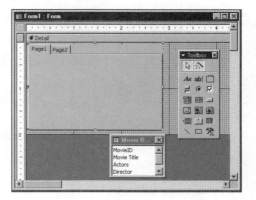

Notes:

- Multiple-tab forms are useful when using forms to create custom dialog boxes that have many options on them. You can use tabs to organize dialog box options into categories.

7 To change the text on the tab:

a. Right-click the tab and select **Properties**. The tab page properties display.

b. Click the **Format** tab.

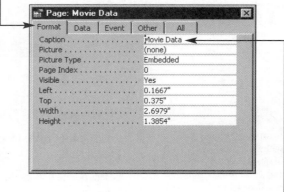

c. Type tab text in the **Caption** property.

d. Press **Enter.**

8 To add another tab if desired, right-click an existing tab and select **Insert Page**. Following is an illustration of a multiple-tab form with three tabs.

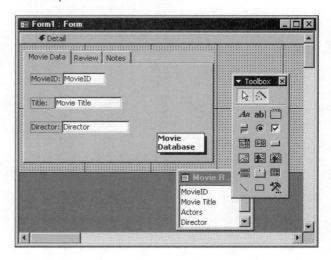

Notes:

- To delete a tab if desired, right-click the tab to delete and select **Delete Page**.

- To move tabs into a different order, right-click a tab and select **Order Pages**.

9 Add fields, controls, and other objects to the form as desired.

10 Press **Ctrl+S** to save the form.

11 Type a name for the form.

12 Click **OK** OK or press **Enter**.

13 Click the **Cancel** button ✕ to close the form.

135

Create a Report Using a Wizard

The Report Wizard prompts you for the information it needs to create a report.

Notes:

• The Report Wizard helps you through creating a report. After you create the report, you can customize it in Design view.

1 Click **Reports** in the Database window.

2 Double-click **Create report by using wizard**. The Report Wizard starts.

3 Select a data source (table or query) for the report.

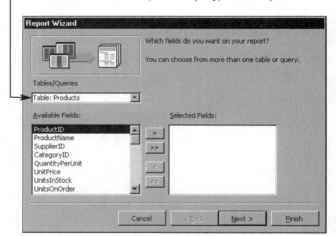

4 Select one or more field(s) to include in the report and click ⊳ .

OR

To add all fields to the report, click ⊳⊳ .

5 Repeat steps 3 and 4 to add another data source if desired.

6 Click the **Next** button Next > .

7 Choose **Layout** and **Orientation** options as desired.

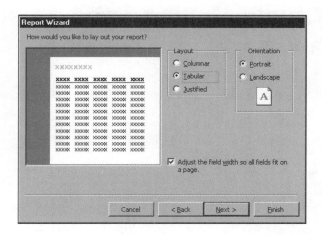

8 At this stage, the Report Wizard screens vary depending on the data source(s) that you selected. Make your choices and click the **Next** button $\boxed{\text{Next >}}$ to continue. The steps in the Report Wizard converge again at the style screen.

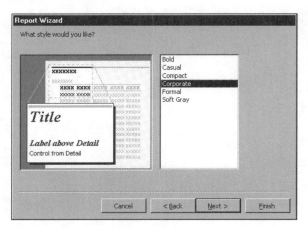

9 Select a style for the report.

10 Click the **Next** button $\boxed{\text{Next >}}$.

11 Type a title for the report.

12 Choose what you want to do next. You can **Preview the report** or **Modify the report's design** by opening it in Design view.

13 Click the **Finish** button $\boxed{\text{Finish}}$.

14 Close the report.

Create Mailing Labels Using a Wizard

Create labels for names and addresses stored in an Access database.

1 Select **Insert**, **Report**. The New Report dialog box opens.

2 Select **Label Wizard**.

3 Select the record source for the labels.

4 Click **OK** [OK]. The Label Wizard starts.

5 Select the label manufacturer.
   *NOTE: If the manufacturer of the labels you will be using is not listed, click the **Customize** button* [Customize...] *and enter measurements and other specifications to create custom labels. You need to enter label specifications such as the size of each label and the number of labels on a page.*

6 Select the label **Product number**.

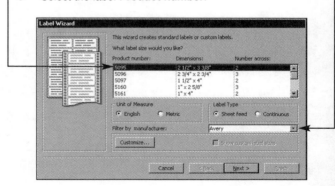

7 Click the **Next** button [Next >].

8 Select the font, font size, and other text formatting for the labels.

9 Click the **Next** button [Next >].

10 Select a field from the record source to add to the label.
   NOTE: Add fields in the order that they will appear on the label.

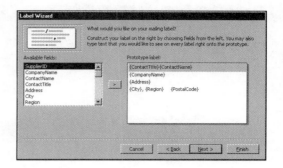

11 Click . The selected field is placed in the label prototype in the right pane.

12 Type any text or spaces if necessary.

NOTE: For example, in the illustration, there is a comma and a space after the City field. A space will need to be added between the ContactTitle and the ContactName fields.

13 Press **Ctrl+Enter** to start a new line if necessary.

14 Repeat steps 10–13 until all fields that you wish to place on the label are added.

15 Click the **Next** button ⎢ Next > ⎢.

16 Select a field to sort on and click ⎢ > ⎢ if you want to print labels in a certain order.

17 Repeat step 16 to sort by multiple fields if desired. For example, you could sort by zip code and then by state.

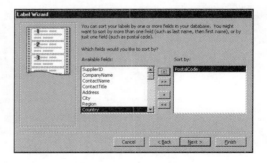

18 Click the **Next** button ⎢ Next > ⎢.

19 Type a name for the label report.

20 Specify whether you want to **See the labels as they will look printed** (shows you a sample label with data) or **Modify the label design** (opens the report in Design view).

21 Click the **Finish** button ⎢ Finish ⎢.

139

Add Page Numbers to a Report

Add a page number field to automatically number report pages.

Insert ➡ Page Numbers...

Notes:

- If you add page numbers to a report using this procedure, Access automatically adds a page header or footer. Page headers and footers print on each page and Access assumes that you want to number every page. If you have already added page headers and footers, it places the page number field in the header or footer as you specify.

- You can add just the page number (example: Page 2) or you can include the number of pages in the document (example: Page 2 of 5).

1 Open the report in Design view.

2 Select **Insert**, **Page Numbers**. The Page Numbers dialog box displays.

3 Select a page number **Format**.

4 Select a **Position**. You can place numbers in the page header or footer.

NOTE: You can move page numbers in Design view after you add them.

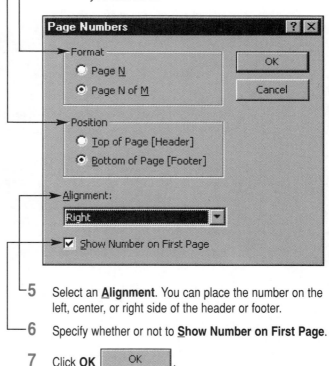

5 Select an **Alignment**. You can place the number on the left, center, or right side of the header or footer.

6 Specify whether or not to **Show Number on First Page**.

7 Click **OK** [OK].

- You can specify whether or not to print the page number on the first page. If the page number might detract from the report title, which appears only on the first page, you can skip printing the page number.

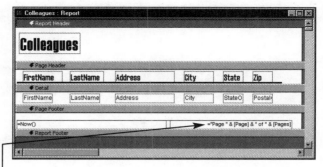

Access inserts a text box that contains a function to add the page number in the format that you selected. In this report, the page number has been added to the Page Footer section.

8   To move the page number, if desired, drag the field.

9   Switch to Print Preview to view your changes.

10   Press the **Save** button ![icon] to save the report design.

11   Click the **Cancel** button ![icon] to close the report when you have finished modifying it.

Create a Data Access Page Using a Wizard

A data access page is a Web page based on database data. The page can be placed on an Internet site or on an intranet.

Notes:

- You can create three types of data access pages:

  1. data entry pages (similar to forms) that accept data

  2. read-only reports where you can filter and otherwise work with the data in Page view but you cannot modify the data

  3. data analysis pages that include analysis tools such as PivotTables and charts

- A data access page can be similar to a form—you can use it to collect data from people who visit your Web site. It can also work like a report—users can sort, filter, and otherwise work with the data source for the page.

1 Click **Insert**, **Page**. The New Data Access Page dialog box opens.

2 Double-click **Page Wizard**. The first Page Wizard screen displays.

3 Select the data source (tables or queries) for the page.

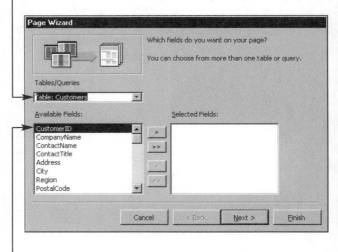

4 Select the fields to add to the page in the **Available Fields** list and click ⟩ .

NOTE: *To select multiple fields, press **Ctrl** and click the next field.*

OR

Click ⟩⟩ to include all of the fields in the record source.

5 Repeat steps 3-4 to add record sources as desired.

6 Click the **Next** button ⟨ Next > ⟩ .

142

- Access comes with a number of themes that you can apply to a page when you create it using the Page Wizard. A theme consists of predesigned formatting styles. For example, a theme includes a background picture, font styles, colors, and other formatting options.

* Data access pages are saved outside the database in the current folder. A shortcut to the page is added to the Database window so that you can open it from within the database.

- Data access pages are stored in HTML files with an .htm extension.

- You must have Internet Explorer version 5.0 or later installed on your computer in order to create or open a data access page.

- You can use the Page Wizard to create a data access page and then modify it in Design view.

7 To set up the page as a read-only report (users cannot edit the database data from the page), group the data. Use the **Grouping Options** button [Grouping Options ...] to further define the layout.

OR

To create a data entry page, skip this step. Do not add a grouping level.

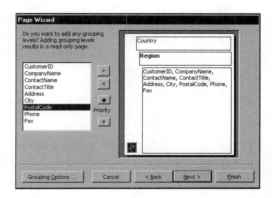

8 Click the **Next** button [Next >].

9 Select a sort order for data if desired.

10 Click the **Next** button [Next >].

11 Enter a title for the data access page.

12 Specify what you wish to do next. You can open the page in Page view (select **Open the page**) or Design view (select **Modify the page's design**).

13 To apply the default theme to the page if desired, select the theme option.

14 Click the **Finish** button [Finish].

143

PowerPoint

Microsoft Office's presentation application helps you to create interactive, self-running, or speaker-controlled visual displays. PowerPoint makes use of multimedia technology to include photographs, drawings, text, graphs, video and audio clips in your presentation. Presentations created in PowerPoint can be used to accompany lectures or as the basis for Web sites. PowerPoint can also be used to create 35-millimeter slides, overhead projections, and printed handouts.

Opening Dialog Box

The Opening Dialog box displays each time you start PowerPoint.

Notes:

- Each option in the Opening Dialog box is covered in further detail within this section of the book.

1   Click to select one of the four Opening Dialog box options:

- The **AutoContent Wizard,** which guides you through creating a new presentation based on the type of information you want to present. It provides content suggestions for getting information across to specific audiences. It also provides pre-designed background and placeholder settings.

- The **Design Template**, which provides a large selection of pre-designed backgrounds and placeholders but does not provide content suggestions.

- The **Blank** presentation, which allows you to add your own content as well as your own background, placeholder, and design choices.
- **Open an existing presentation**, which allows you to open a presentation that has already been created.

2   Click **OK** | OK | to create or open a presentation.

OR

Click **Cancel** | Cancel | to close the dialog box and get a blank PowerPoint screen.

PowerPoint Screen in Normal View

It is important to become familiar with the main PowerPoint screen features that are displayed in Normal view.

Notes:

- The Slide view window shows a slide as it will be shown in Slide Show view—with backgrounds and pictures, etc.

- Any text that is added to a place-holder is reflected in the Outline view window.

Normal view is PowerPoint's default view. It splits the screen into three windows: Outline, Slide, and Notes. In this view all aspects of one slide are displayed at once.

1   The top bar is the **Title bar**. A temporary title (Presentations1) appears within brackets until you save and name the presentation file.

2   The **Application Control buttons**, which are located on the right side of the Title bar, allow you to control how the PowerPoint application will appear onscreen.

- Click the **Minimize** button ▬ to reduce the application window to an icon on the Windows' Taskbar at the bottom of your screen.

- Click the **Restore Window** button ⊡ to restore the application window.
OR
Click the **Mazimize** button ☐ to maximize the application window.

- Click the **Close** button ✖ to close PowerPoint.

3   The second bar is the **Menu bar**. It provides drop-down menus that contain PowerPoint commands. Click on a desired menu item to reveal the available commands.

4   The **Document Control buttons**, which are located on the right side of the Menu bar, allow you to control how the current PowerPoint presentation will appear onscreen.

- Click the **Mimimize** button ▬ to reduce the presentation to an icon at the bottom of the PowerPoint application window.

- Click the **Restore Window** button ⊡ to restore the presentation window to its previous size and location.
OR
Click the **Maximize** button ☐ to maximize the presentation window.

NORMAL VIEW

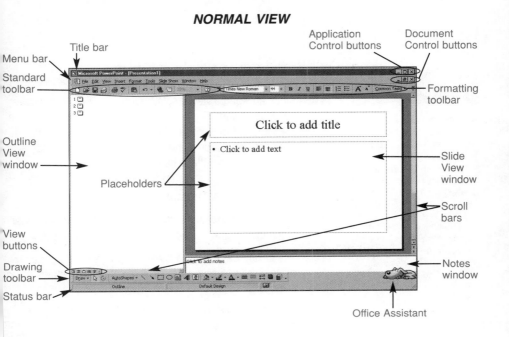

Menu bar
Title bar
Application Control buttons
Document Control buttons
Standard toolbar
Formatting toolbar
Outline View window
Placeholders
Slide View window
Scroll bars
View buttons
Drawing toolbar
Status bar
Click to add title
• Click to add text
Notes window
Office Assistant

---

5 Click the **Close** button ❌ to close the presentation.

6 The **Standard toolbar** contains shortcut buttons that access PowerPoint's most commonly used commands, such as Print, Save, and E-Mail.

7 The **Formatting toolbar** contains shortcut buttons that allow you to adjust the way objects and text appear on the screen and in presentations.

8 **Placeholders** are empty text or graphics boxes provided as prompts. Each prompt indicates what type of text or graphic should be inserted. The type of slide layout that you select will determine which placeholders will be present.

NOTE: Slide layouts will be discussed further in this section of the book.

9 **Scroll bars** allow you to scroll through each window to view its full contents.

149

PowerPoint Screen in Normal View

(continued)

Notes:

- Most buttons of the Standard and Formatting toolbars are similar or identical to buttons available in other Office 2000 applications.

- The Office Assistant will often jump into action on its own whenever it senses that it can help you with a function.

10 Although Normal view displays **Outline view**, **Slide view**, and **Notes view** windows simultaneously, you can also use the **View buttons** to change the screen to display only one view at a time. Slide Sorter and Slide Show views may also be accessed from these buttons.

NOTE: Each slide view will be discussed further in this section of the book.

11 The **Drawing toolbar** contains buttons which access most of the tools you will need to add graphics to your slides.

12 The **status bar** identifies the number of the slide currently being displayed as well as the template design that is being used.

13 The **Office Assistant** is an animated helper. Click on the assistant whenever you need help.

Continue

Design Templates

Design Templates are pre-designed presentations that contain a wide variety of stylish designs such as coordinating backgrounds, fonts, colors, objects, etc. PowerPoint provides numerous professionally designed templates so that you can focus on your presentation's content instead of its design.

Notes:

- Design Templates can also be selected from the PowerPoint Opening dialog box when you start the application.

- The same AutoLayout options available when creating a blank presentation are provided when creating a presentation from a Design Template.

- A template contains only design information. It does not contain content or content prompts.

- Template designs are applied to all slides within a presentation.

- You cannot select more than one Design Template per presentation. However, you can alter individual slides as desired.

- The Office 97 Templates tab is available if you previously had Office 97 installed on your computer. This tab allows you to choose from templates that were provided in Office 97.

Select a Design Template for a New Presentation

1 Click **File**, **New** to open the New Presentation dialog box.

2 Click the **Design Templates** tab to bring it to the front.

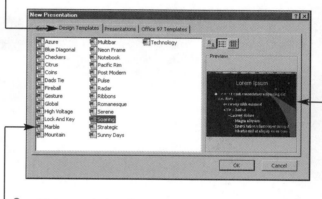

3 Click on a desired Design Template and a preview of the template will appear on the right side of the dialog box.
NOTE: If the template you select is not installed, a prompt will appear asking you to click ***OK*** [OK] *to install it.*

4 Click **OK** [OK] to use the selected Design Template in your new presentation.

Change the Design Template for an Existing Presentation

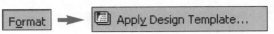

1   Open the presentation that you want to change.

2   Click **Format**, **Apply Design Template** to open the Apply Design Template dialog box.

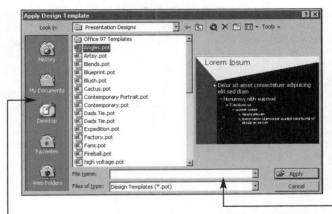

3   A list of available template names is listed in the middle of the dialog box and a preview window is presented on the right.

4   To select a template, click on a Design Template file.

OR

Double-click the Office 97 folder and click on an Office 97 template.

OR

Click to select any of the folders listed on the left side of the dialog box and then click on a desired file.

OR

Type the name of file you wish to use in the **File name** text box.

5   Click the **Apply** button to apply the selected template to the presentation.

OR

Click the **Cancel** button to exit the dialog box without applying a new template.

153

AutoContent Wizard

The AutoContent Wizard steps you through a series of questions relating to the information you wish to present and then formats a content-driven presentation based on your responses. The result is a powerful template with content prompts that will help you build a professional-quality presentation.

1   Click **File**, **New** to open the New Presentation dialog box.

2   Click the **General** tab to bring it to the front.

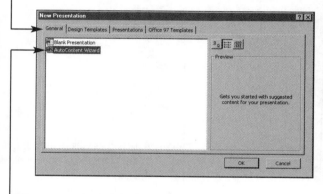

3   Double-click the **AutoContent Wizard** icon to start the wizard.

4   Click the **Next** button Next > on the first wizard screen to begin building the presentation.

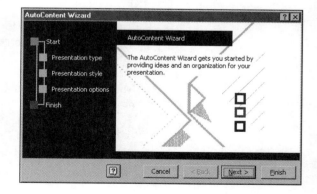

- If you select a presentation choice that is not currently installed in your system, you will be prompted to provide the disk or CD-ROM that contains the file.

- To remove template choices from the wizard, click the **Remove** button on the second screen, select the presentation(s) to be removed, and click **OK**.

5 On the second wizard screen, click a button that best describes the category of the presentation type you wish to give.

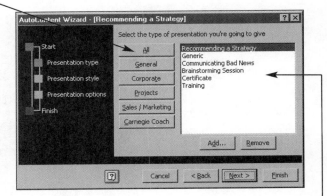

6 Select a presentation type from the window on the right and click the **Next** button [Next >].

7 On the third wizard screen, select the style and format for your presentation and click the **Next** button [Next >].

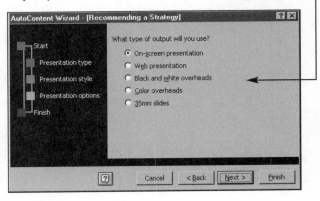

155

8   On the fourth wizard screen, enter the presentation title
and footer text, select the date and slide number check
boxes if desired, and click the **Next** button Next > .

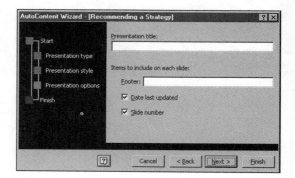

9   Click the **Finish** button Finish once you have supplied
all the necessary information for the presentation.

OR

If necessary, click the **Back** button < Back to revise
any information provided on the previous screens.

OR

Click the **Cancel** button Cancel to exit the wizard
without creating a new presentation.

10   When the wizard is complete, the presentation displays
in Normal view. From the Outline view window, you can
read the suggested text prompts, which will guide you by
providing relevant text for the type of presentation you
wish to give.

Continue ➡

Slide Sorter View

Slide Sorter view displays every slide within a presentation in miniature view. This allows you to see the entire flow of your presentation and also allows you to make some universal changes to all slides or selected slides if desired.

Notes:

- It is easiest to move and copy slides within Slide Sorter view because you can see the results immediately.

- Press and hold the **Ctrl** key while clicking to select more than one slide at a time in Slide Sorter view.

- The keyboard shortcut for cutting slides (for moving to a new location) is **Ctrl+X**.

- The keyboard shortcut for copying slides is **Ctrl+C**.

1　Click **View**, **Slide Sorter**.

　OR

　Click the **Slide Sorter** button ⊞ at the bottom of the screen.

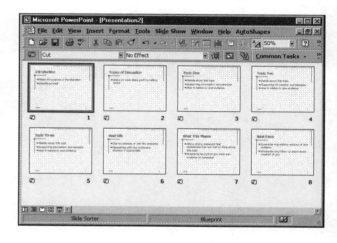

2　**To change the order of the existing slides:**

　a. Click on the slide you want to move.

　b. Drag it to a new location.

Notes:

- The keyboard shortcut for pasting slides is **Ctrl+V**.

- To undo a slide deletion, click the

  Undo button ⟲ ▾ immediately. The slide will be restored.

3 **To copy a slide:**

   a. Click on the slide you want to copy.

   b. Click **Edit**, **Copy**.

   OR

   Click the **Copy** button ▣ on the Standard toolbar.

   c. Click to the right of the new slide location.

   d. Click **Edit**, **Paste**.

   OR

   Click the **Paste** button ▣ on the Standard toolbar.

4 **To delete a slide in Slide Sorter view:**

   a. Click on the slide you want to delete.

   b. Press the **Delete** key.

   OR

   Click **Edit**, **Delete Slide**.

5 **To insert a new slide:**

   a. Position cursor to the left of the new slide location.

   b. Click **Insert**, **New Slide**.

   c. Choose an **AutoLayout**.

   d. Click **OK** ▢ OK ▢.

6 To exit Slide Sorter view, click another view option on the **View** menu or from the view buttons at the bottom of the screen.

159

Background

Different colors, patterns, and textures can be added to the background of one slide, select slides, or to an entire presentation. Changing a default background can create interesting and eye-catching results.

1 With a slide selected, click **Format**, **Background** to open the background dialog box.

2 The **Background fill** box shows a preview of how your slide(s) will look with a particular fill.

3 To change the background colors or texture, click on the **Background fill** drop-down arrow.

4 Select **More Colors** from the drop-down list if you wish to change the preselected color scheme.

5 Select **Fill Effects** from the drop-down list if you wish to change the texture of the background. The Fill Effects dialog box has four tabs:
- **Gradient** provides different variegated effects.
- **Texture** provides numerous textures, from marble to a crumpled-up paper bag. Each texture can be previewed in the preview box.

160

• Using too many textures, patterns, or pictures within your presentation can be distracting.

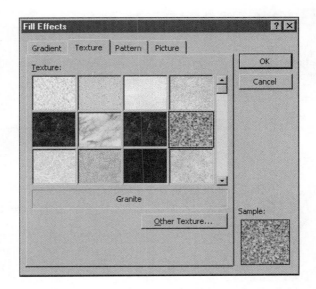

• **Pattern** provides options such as plaid and bricks. The pattern color can also be changed here.

• **Picture** inserts a picture as a background for a slide. Click **Select Picture** on this tab to access many of the pictures that come preloaded with PowerPoint.

6 Click **Preview** to see what the slide will look like with the selected background.

7 If desired, choose **Omit background graphics from master**. If this option is selected, the formatting that you choose will not be entered on the Master Slide.

8 Click the **Apply to All** button [Apply to All] to apply the background settings to the entire presentation.

OR

Click the **Apply** button [Apply] to apply the background settings only to the selected slide or slides.

OR

Click the **Cancel** button [Cancel] to return to the presentation without making any changes.

Slide Layout

The Slide Layout feature allows you to change the layout of a slide as well as to choose a layout for a new slide. The slide layout determines how title, subtitle, text, picture, and chart placeholders will appear on the screen.

Notes:

- You may adjust placeholder text and borders as desired after choosing a slide layout. In Slide view, simply click on a placeholder and select new formatting options.

- You can move a placeholder by clicking on it and dragging it to a new position.

- To change a placeholder's size, click on a placeholder handle and drag to enlarge or reduce it.

- All placeholder formatting and adjusting will only affect the current slide.

1 Click **Format**, **Slide Layout**.

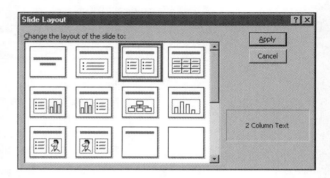

2 The layout for the current slide is highlighted in the Slide Layout dialog box, and the name of the layout is listed in the bottom-right corner.

3 **To select a new slide layout option for the current slide:**
   - Click on a new slide layout option and click the **Apply** button **Apply**.

   OR

   To reapply the default master slide layout after formatting or adjusting placeholders on the current slide:

   - Click the **Reapply** button **Reapply**.

   OR

   Click the **Cancel** button **Cancel** to return to the presentation without changing the layout of the current slide.

Continue

Slide Master

The slide master acts as a pattern for all slides within a presentation except for the title slide (which may be adjusted separately). Any formatting or adjusting of placeholders, background patterns, etc. that is applied to the slide master will affect all current and future slides in a presentation.

Notes:

- Other Master patterns are also available under the **View**, **Master** menu. The **title master** acts as a pattern for all title slides within a presentation, the **handouts master** acts as a pattern for handouts, and the **notes master** acts as a pattern for all notes pages.

- Any changes you make to a master will automatically reformat the remaining slides in the presentation.

- To make changes to individual slides (so that not all slides within a presentation are affected), select placeholders within Slide view and make adjustments.

1   Click **View**, **Master**, **Slide Master** to view the Master layout.

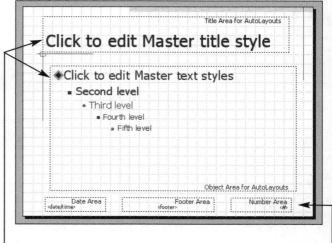

2   To move placeholders for all slides within the presentation, click and drag to the desired location.

3   To make formatting changes to a placeholder for all slides within the presentation, click on the placeholder and make font, font size, font color, tab adjustments, etc.

4   To make changes to the background template, click on the various objects and move, delete, or adjust them as desired.

5   To adjust the Date, Footer, or Slide Number areas, click on the appropriate placeholder and make the desired adjustments.

164

- Each background template is made up of various drawing objects. In Slide Master view, you can click on a piece of the background to delete, move, or adjust it.

6 When you are finished adjusting the slide master, click the **Close** button on the Master toolbar to exit slide master view and return to the previous view.

OR

Click **View** and select another view.

OR

Click on a view button at the bottom of the screen.

Headers and Footers

A header contains information that appears at the top of a PowerPoint note page or handout. A footer contains information that appears at the bottom of a slide, note page, or handout. Header and footer information can include date, time, slide number, and/or additional text.

Notes:

- You can apply only footers to slides; you cannot apply headers. You can apply headers to notes and handouts, however.

- Footers can be set to appear on an individual slide, select slides, or on all slides within a presentation.

Insert Footers on Slides

1 Click **View**, **Header and Footer**.

2 The Header and Footer dialog box displays with the Slide tab selected by default.

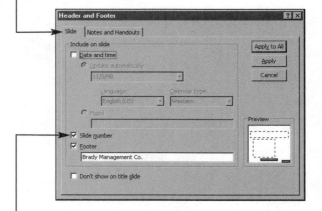

3 Click **Date and time** to access the date and/or time options, which may be used to insert the date into the footer.

4 Click **Slide number** to insert the slide number into the footer.

5 If desired, select the **Footer** check box to access the footer text box. This option allows you to add a line of text.

6 Click **Don't show on title slide** if you want to apply footers to all slides except for the initial title slide.

7 Click the **Apply to All** button Apply to All to apply footer information to all slides in the current presentation.

OR

Click the **Apply** button 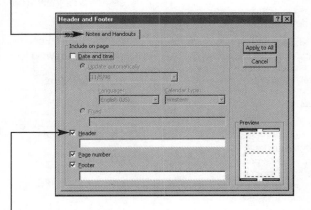 Apply to apply footer information to the selected slides only.

OR

Click the **Cancel** button Cancel to return to the presentation without inserting any footer information.

Notes:

- Headers and Footers are applied to every page when inserting them into notes pages and handouts.

- On notes and handout pages, date and time information is displayed in the header, not in the footer.

- A line of header text may only be added to Notes or Handouts. It can not be inserted into slides.

- Use the Preview window to review the placement of header and footer items you are selecting.

Insert Headers and/or Footers on Notes and Handouts

1   Click **View**, **Header and Footer**.

2   When the Header and Footer dialog box displays, click the Notes and Handouts tab.

3   Click **Date and time** to access the date and/or time options, which may be used to insert the date into the header of each notes page and handout.

4   Click the **Header** check box to access the header text box. This option allows you to add a line of text at the top of each note page and handout.

5   Click the **Footer** check box to access the footer text box. This option allows you to add a line of text at the bottom of each notes page and handout.

6   Click the **Apply to All** button Apply to All to apply header and footer formatting to all slides in the current presentation.

OR

Click the **Cancel** button Cancel to return to the presentation without inserting any header or footer formatting to the slides.

Draw Objects

The PowerPoint drawing tools allow you to draw objects using various predefined shapes, colors, and effects.

Notes:

- You can create drawing objects in Slide view only.

- To draw a perfect square or circle, press and hold the **Shift** key as you drag to create the shape.

- To draw several objects using the same drawing tool, double-click on a desired Drawing toolbar button and click to draw. Each time you release the mouse, the cursor is prepared to create another shape.

- The **Select** button

   activates Select mode, which enables you to select drawing objects on the screen.

Draw a Shape

1 If necessary, click **View**, **Toolbars**, **Drawing** to display the Drawing toolbar.

2 In Slide view, click on one of the four drawing tools available on the Drawing toolbar:

    Line tool

   Arrow tool

   Rectangle tool

   Oval tool

3 Click on the slide and drag to create the desired shape.

Change the Shape of a Drawing

1 Click on the drawing object.

2 To select more than one drawing object at a time, press the **Shift** key as you click on each object.

3 Each selected drawing object is surrounded by four to eight handles (small squares).

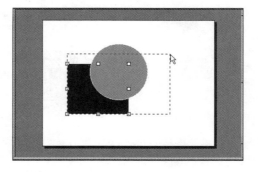

4 Click on any handle and drag inward to reduce the size of the object(s) or outward to enlarge it.

Notes:

- To retain the original proportions of a drawing object while reducing or enlarging it, use a corner handle (not a middle handle) while pressing the **Shift** key as you drag to resize it.

- Many of the drawing features in PowerPoint are the same as those used in other Microsoft applications, such as Word 2000.

Move a Drawing

1 Click inside of a drawing object to select it.

2 To select more than one object at a time, press the **Shift** key as you click on each object.

3 Click and drag the object(s) to the desired location.

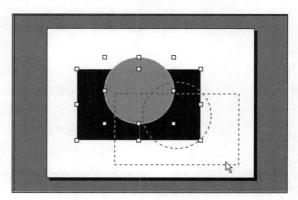

Copy a Drawing

1 Click on the drawing object.

2 To select more than one drawing object at a time, use the **Shift** key as you click on each object.

3 Do the following:

a. Click **Edit**, **Copy**.

b. Place the cursor where you wish to paste the copied object(s).

OR

a. Press the **Ctrl** key.

b. Drag the mouse to a desired location on the same slide and a copy of the object(s) will appear when you release the mouse.

169

Group Objects

The Group option allows you to combine several objects into one.

Notes:

- Grouping can save you a lot of time and energy. Once objects are grouped, they can be resized, moved, and copied as though they were one object.

- To edit individual objects within a group, you must first ungroup the object.

- To ungroup a grouped object, right-click on the object and click **Grouping**, **Ungroup**. Or, click the **Draw** button on the Drawing toolbar and click **Grouping**, **Ungroup**.

1 Click an object on a slide.

2 Press and hold the **Shift** key and select the additional items you want to group.

3 Handles will appear around each object.

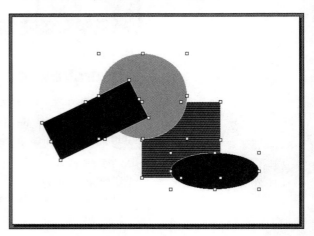

4 Right-click on the grouped objects and select **Grouping** from the shortcut menu.

OR

Click the **Draw** button Draw ▾ on the Drawing toolbar.

5 Click the **Group** button ⊞ Group .

6 One set of handles now surrounds the entire grouped object.

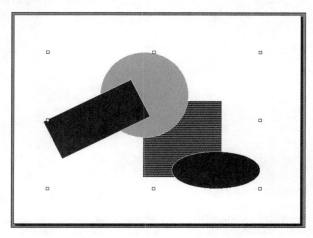

7 Size, move, and/or copy the grouped object as desired.

Order Objects

The Order option allows you to change how objects are layered on a slide by sending them backward or forward in the order.

1 Click one object on a slide whose order you want to change.

2 Selection handles will indicate the selected object.

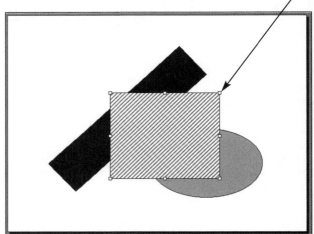

3 Click the **Draw** button Draw ▾ on the Drawing toolbar.

OR

Right-click to access a shortcut menu.

4 Click **Order**.

5 Select an order option from the submenu that displays:

- Click the **Send Backward** button ⬛ Send Backward to move the object back one layer at a time.

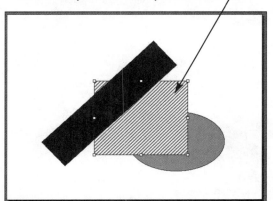

- Click the **Send to Back** button ⬛ Send to Back to move the object to the back of all other objects in the order.

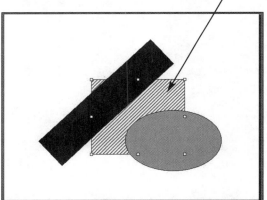

- Click the **Bring Forward** button ⬛ Bring Forward to move the object forward one layer at a time.

- Click the **Bring to Front** button ⬛ Bring to Front to move the object to the front of all other objects in the order.

173

Charts

The PowerPoint Chart feature can be used to illustrate data in a graphic display.

Notes:

- If the **Chart** button
  is not available on the Standard toolbar, click the **More Buttons** button
  to reveal it.

- If you select the Chart and Text or Text and Chart layout for a new slide, you can double-click on the Chart placeholder to launch chart options.

- The Datasheet window is not displayed on the slide during Slide Show view or when printing. To display Datasheet information on the slide, click the **Data Table** button
  on the Standard toolbar (while in Chart mode) and the information will be added below the chart illustration.

1 From Slide view, click **Insert**, **Chart**.

   OR

   Click the **Chart** button on the Standard toolbar.

2 A sample chart appears on the slide along with a Datasheet window containing sample data.

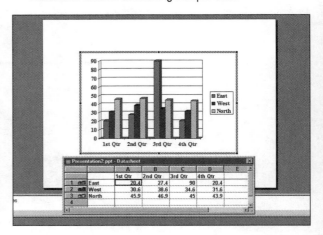

3 To erase the sample data, highlight the information in the Datasheet window and press the **Delete** key.

4 Type your own information into the Datasheet. Note that the chart changes to reflect the new data.

174

Notes:

- When a chart is selected, the buttons on the Formatting toolbar change to enable you to format numbers on the Datasheet.

5   Note that the Standard toolbar has changed to include various charting options:

- The **Chart Area** drop-down menu

  `Chart Area` ▼ indicates which chart object is currently selected for editing. Click the drop-down arrow to select another chart object.

- The **Format Chart Areas** button accesses the Format Chart Area dialog box, which allows you to adjust the color, pattern, and font for the selected chart object.

- The **Import File** button allows you to import a spreadsheet from another program.

- The **View Datasheet** button brings the Datasheet window into view if it is hidden.

- The **By Row** button displays all data by row.

- The **By Column** button displays all data by column.

- The **Data Table** button adds a datasheet inside the chart illustration so that it may be viewed on the slide.

- The **Chart Type drop-down** button allows you to change the current chart type (to pie, area, line, etc.).

- The **Category Access Gridlines** button adds vertical grid lines to the chart.

- The **Value Access Gridlines** button adds horizontal grid lines to the chart.

- The **Legend** button adds a legend to the chart.

- The **Drawing** button displays the Drawing toolbar.

6   After formatting a chart, click away from it to return to your presentation.

7   Move the chart to desired location.

Organization Charts

Organization charts provide a simple visual for displaying hierarchical information, such as a list of supervisors, managers, and reporting staff. PowerPoint uses the Microsoft Organization Chart application to create a organization chart as a slide object.

Notes:

- You can also create an organization chart by selecting the Organization Chart layout option when creating a new slide. Double-click on the organization chart placeholder and follow the steps listed on the right.

- When you create an organization chart using the Microsoft Organization Chart application, the chart is saved as an object within the presentation. It is not saved as a separate file.

1 Click **Insert**, **Picture**, **Organization Chart**, or insert a new slide with the Organization Chart layout. If you choose the second method, double-click on the lower box to insert the chart. In either case, MS Organization Chart will open.

2 When MS Organization Chart opens, a number of boxes are already displayed. Click in each one to replace the placeholder text with your information.

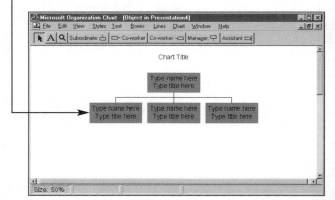

3 Use the toolbar buttons to add new boxes to the chart. Select the desired relationship from the toolbar and then click on the appropriate boxes in the chart.

- Subordinate: ⌐ will add a new box immediately below the selected box.

- ⌐:Co-worker will add new boxes to the immediate left and right, respectively, of the selected box.

- Manager: ⌐ will add a new box immediately above the selected box.

- Assistant: ⌐ will add a branched box below the selected box.

176

Notes:

- You can change chart colors by changing the fill color of the Color Scheme dialog box.

4   Click the **Text** tool 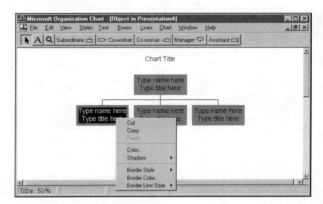 to change the font of the displayed text.

5   Click on the **Zoom** tool to zoom in and out of the display.

6   Right-clicking on any box in the chart or selecting **Boxes** from the menu allows you to format a selected box or boxes.

7   The last three options above can also be applied to selected chart lines by right-clicking any line or selecting **Lines** from the menu.

8   You can select text font, color, and alignment by using the **Text** menu.

9   The **Styles** menu provides a choice of layouts for the chart.

10 Click **File**, **Close and Return to Presentation** to close MS Organization Chart. A dialog box will ask you if you wish to update before closing the chart. Click **Yes** to insert the chart into your presentation, or **No** to return to your presentation without inserting the chart. (Clicking **No** will also delete the chart.)

11 To edit a chart, simply double-click on it, and MS Organization Chart will re-open.

Save as Web Page

PowerPoint's Save as Web Page feature makes it very easy to save a presentation as an HTML document so that it can be used as a Web page on the World Wide Web or on a company intranet.

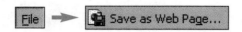

Notes:

- HTML stands for Hypertext Markup Language.

- Most PowerPoint fonts and styles are prepared for HTML usage. Therefore, once you save a presentation as a Web page, little—if any—reformatting should have to take place.

- Always preview your Web page in a Web Browser prior to publishing it on the Internet or on an intranet. Some items may adjust or appear slightly askew, depending on the Web browser you are using.

1 Open or create a presentation.

2 Click **File**, **Save as Web Page**.

3 In the Save as dialog box the file type will automatically be set to **Web Page (*.htm; *.html)** in the **Save as type** box. This will allow the file to be read across different operating systems.

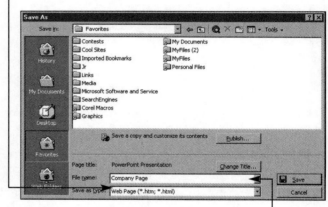

4 Click in the **File name** box and type a name.

5 Click the **Save** button.

178

Continue ➡

Hyperlinks

PowerPoint allows you to create hyperlinks in your presentation that can link viewers to Web pages, other files, or other slides in the current presentation.

Notes:

- The keyboard shortcut for inserting a hyperlink is **Ctrl+K**.

- A Web address is also called a URL (Uniform Resource Locator).

- Hyperlinks use HTTP (Hypertext Transfer Protocol) to link images and text.

- The **Create New Document** option in the Insert Hyperlink dialog box allows you to create a new PowerPoint document and assign a link to it at the same time.

- The **E-mail address** option in the Insert Hyperlink dialog box allows you to create a link to an e-mail address.

Link to a Web Page or File

1 In Slide or Outline view, select a string of text within a placeholder or text box.

   OR

   Select a slide object, such as a picture, clip art image, or button created with AutoShapes or other drawing tools.

2 Click **Insert**, **Hyperlink** to access the Insert Hyperlink dialog box.

3 Click the **Existing File or Web Page** button .

4 In the **Type the file** or **Web page name** text box, type the Web page address or the name and system location of a file to which you want to link.

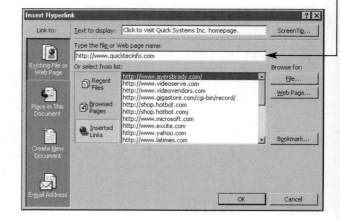

180

OR

— Click on a shortcut list to choose from and click on a
recently accessed Web site or file.

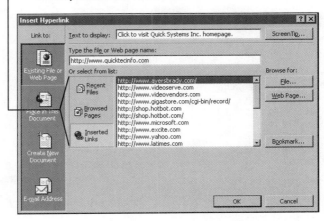

OR

Click the **Web Page** button [Web Page...] to select a
Web page on the Internet or on a connected intranet.

OR

Click the **File** button [File...] to select a file on
your system, on disk, or on a connected network.

5 Click **OK** [OK] to insert the hyperlink on the
selected slide.

6 If text was used to create the hyperlink, it will now be
underlined and appear in a different color to indicate that
it is a link.

Hyperlinks

(continued)

Notes:

- Hyperlinks can be assigned to a string of text (within a placeholder or text box) or to a slide object such as a button, picture, or clip art.

- Hyperlinks can be created in Slide or Outline view. However, they can only be activated while a slide show is running.

Link to Another Slide in Current Presentation

1 From Slide or Outline view, select a string of text within a placeholder or text box.

OR

Select a slide object—such as a picture, clip art image, or button—created with AutoShapes or other drawing tools.

2 Click **Insert**, **Hyperlink** to access the Insert Hyperlink dialog box.

3 Click the **Place in this Document** button and select a slide in the current presentation.

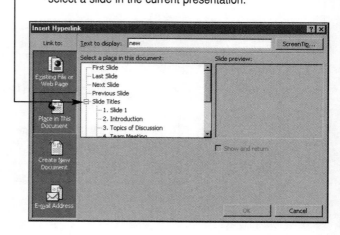

OR

a. Click the **Existing File or Web Page** button .

b. Click the **Bookmark** button 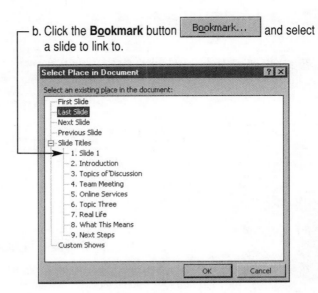 and select a slide to link to.

4   Click **OK** [OK] to accept the slide.

5   Click **OK** [OK] to insert the hyperlink onto the selected slide.

Web Page Preview

The Web Page Preview option allows you to preview a PowerPoint document that has been saved as an HTML file by launching a Web browser application.

Notes:

- If you are experiencing difficulties previewing your Web page, try starting your browser application page prior to selecting **File**, **Web Page Preview**.

- Prior to publishing a presentation on the Internet or on an intranet, always preview it through more than one browser application. Some items may appear slightly askew, depending on the Web browser you are using. Minor adjustments may be required.

- Contact your Internet service provider or network administrator (if you're using an intranet) for more specifics about launching the Web page you've created.

1 Save a presentation as an HTML file (see *Save as Web Page*).

2 Click **File**, **Web Page Preview**.

3 Your system's default Web browser application will start and the current presentation will be displayed in the application window.

4 The title of each slide in the presentation is listed on the left.

5 Each title is a hyperlink. Click on a title to be "linked" to the specified slide.

184

Continue

Transitions

Transitions are the special effects that take place while moving from one slide to the next during a slide show.

Notes:

In Slide View or Outline View

1   Click **Slide Show**, **Slide Transition**.

2   The **Effect** box contains a picture to demonstrate the transition effects before they are set.

3   Click the drop-down list [Blinds Vertical ▼] to select an effect.

4   Choose a speed by clicking the appropriate option button.

5   Choose when the slide should make the transition: either **Automatically** after a set amount of time, or **On mouse click**.

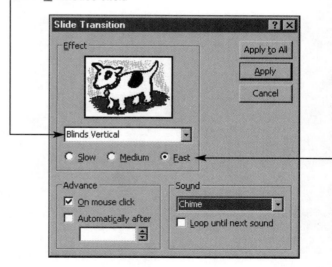

6   Click the **Sound** drop-down list box [Chime ▼] to apply a sound to the transition. (The sound can only be heard if the computer running the slide show has the appropriate hardware.)

Notes:

- Transitions may be applied in any view. However, applying them in Slide Sorter view is fastest and easiest.

- Select multiple slides that will receive the same transition effects in Slide Sorter view by holding down the **Shift** key while clicking each slide.

7 Click the **Apply to All** button Apply to All to apply the transition settings to the entire presentation.

OR

Click the **Apply** button Apply to apply the transition settings only to the selected slide(s).

OR

Click the **Cancel** button Cancel to return to the presentation without applying a transition.

From Slide Sorter View

1 In Slide Sorter view, the Slide Sorter toolbar includes

a **Slide Transition** button . Click on it and the Slide Transition dialog box will open.

2 On the Slide Sorter toolbar, you can also change or add a transition by clicking on the **Slide Transition Effects** drop-down list to select an effect. The Slide Transition dialog box will not open, however, so you cannot set timing or sound.

Preset Animation

PowerPoint's Animation feature enables you to animate the appearance of specified objects and text during a slide show presentation. PowerPoint's Preset Animation option provides you with fourteen animation settings to choose from.

Notes:

- Animation effects can only be viewed in full while a slide show is running. However, a preview of the animation setting may be viewed within Slide Sorter view by clicking the animation icon that appears under the slide miniature.

- In earlier versions of PowerPoint, the Animation feature was referred to as the "Builds feature."

1 To animate objects one at a time on a slide, click on an object while in Slide view.

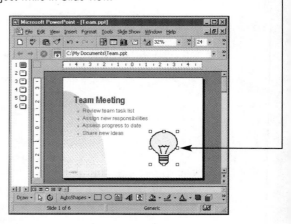

2 To animate several objects on a slide at once, using the same animation effect, select one or more slides in Slide Sorter view.

NOTE: Only placeholders and background objects will receive animation effects. Additional objects added to slides must be animated seperately (see step 1).

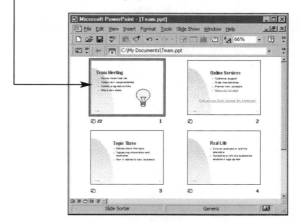

188

3   Click **Slide Show, Preset Animation** and choose one of the following animation options from the submenu that displays:

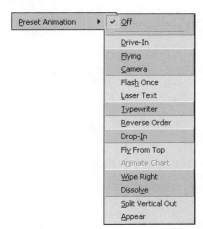

4   To view the animation effect, click **Slide Show, Animation Preview**.

Turn Animation Off

1   To turn animation off, select the animated object(s) in Slide view.

OR

Select the entire slide in Slide Sorter view.

NOTE: If you assign preset animation to objects individually, you must remove those effects individually in Slide view.

2   Click **Slide Show, Preset Animation**.

3   Click the **Off** option.

189

Slide Show Viewing

Once your presentation is complete and all slide show enhancements have been set, you are ready to display the show. PowerPoint provides several ways to view slide show transitions, animation, and other effects.

Notes:

- The keyboard shortcut for launching into Slide Show view is **F5**.

- To exit a slide show while it is still running, press the **Esc** key or right-click on any slide and click **End Show** on the shortcut menu.

Preview Individual Slide Effects in Miniature Window

1   In Slide or Outline view, place insertion point within a desired slide.

2   Click **Slide Show**, **Animation Preview**.

3   A miniature window will appear and display all special effects assigned to the selected slide.

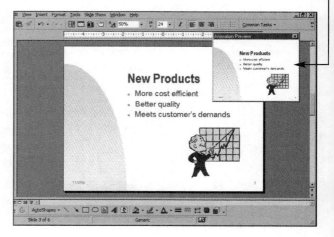

4   To view another slide's settings, click on another slide.

Preview Individual Slide Effects on a Full Screen

1   In Slide or Outline view, place cursor within a desired slide.

2   Click the **Slide Show View** button ☰ at the bottom of the screen.

3   The slide show will run from the selected slide forward if you click the mouse or press the arrow keys on the keyboard.

View Entire Slide Show from the Beginning

1   Open a presentation.

2   From any view or any selected slide, click **Sli<u>d</u>e Show**, **<u>V</u>iew Show**.

OR

Click **<u>V</u>iew**, **Slide Sho<u>w</u>**.

3   Click the mouse to advance through the slide show.

OR

Use the **Up** or **Right arrow keys** on the keyboard to move forward and the **Down** or **Left arrow keys** to repeat a slide or to repeat the animation effect of an object or text item.

OR

If slide timings have been set, the presentation will advance automatically.

Outlook

Microsoft Office's scheduling and organization application provides you with a calendar, journal, contact list, task list, and notes. Outlook also creates and manages e-mail, either through an online service or through a workplace network.

Outlook's components are fully integrated, so that you can send an e-mail scheduling a meeting, for example, and the appointment will automatically show up on your calendar.

Outlook is particularly useful in a networked environment, where it can serve to coordinate the activities of those who use it. It can be used to find mutually convenient times to schedule meetings, for instance, or to assign tasks to team members and track their progress.

Use the Folder List

Perform simple file management tasks without leaving Outlook. Use the Folder List to work with the contents of both Outlook folders and any other folders on your hard disk.

Notes:

- Open, copy, delete, and otherwise manage files without leaving Outlook.

- File management in Outlook is similar to file management in Windows Explorer. Right-click files and folders to open a shortcut menu with file operation commands such as printing, copying, moving, etc.

1 Click **View**, **Folder List** if necessary to display the Folder List. The Folder List shows the contents of the current folder.

2 To view the contents of a folder, click the folder in the Folder List.

Example: If you are in Outlook, the Folder List shows Outlook folders. The Outlook window shows the items in the current folder. This illustration shows the contents of the Deleted Items folder because Deleted Items is selected in the Folder List.

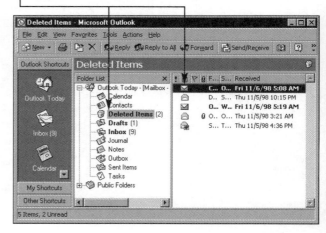

- You can remove fields in the Outlook window (such as the file type) to make more room on the screen. Right-click the column heading and click **Remove This Column**.

3 To display the contents of folders outside of Outlook on your hard disk:

a. Click the **Other Shortcuts** button [Other Shortcuts] on the Outlook Bar.

b. Click the folder or drive you want to view in the Folders group on the Outlook Bar. Outlook displays the contents of the selected folder or drive in the Folder List.

c. In the Folder List, click the drive or folder you want to view. The contents of the selected drive or folder are displayed in the Outlook window.

*NOTE: To view the contents of a folder in a second window, right-click the folder and click **Open**.*

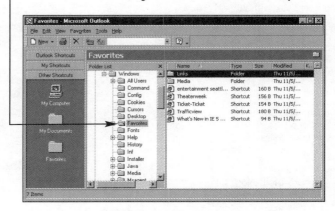

4 Use the same techniques that you use in Windows Explorer to manage files.

Examples: Right-click a file and select from the shortcut menu to copy, delete, or rename. Drag a file to another folder to move it.

195

Use the Outlook Bar

Use the Outlook Bar, located on the left side of the Outlook window, to navigate between Outlook components.

Notes:

- You can also use the Outlook Bar to display folders and files on your computer without leaving Outlook. You can add shortcuts to folders to the Outlook Bar.

- The Outlook Bar has three separate groups of icons. The Outlook Shortcuts group is used to switch between Outlook components.

- Click the **My Shortcuts** button on the Outlook Bar to display My Shortcuts icons.

- The My Shortcuts group shows the default folders in the Mail component. You can create folders in Mail and move mail messages from the Inbox to a folder to organize your Mail.

- You can add to the My Shortcuts group any shortcuts to folders that you create.

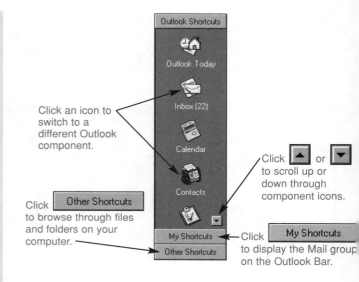

Click an icon to switch to a different Outlook component.

Click **Other Shortcuts** to browse through files and folders on your computer.

Click ▲ or ▼ to scroll up or down through component icons.

Click **My Shortcuts** to display the Mail group on the Outlook Bar.

My Shortcuts

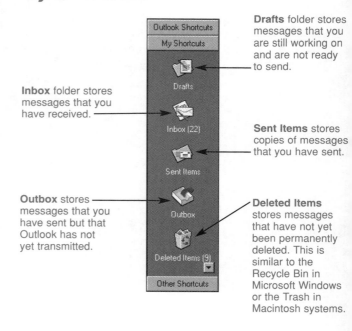

Inbox folder stores messages that you have received.

Outbox stores messages that you have sent but that Outlook has not yet transmitted.

Drafts folder stores messages that you are still working on and are not ready to send.

Sent Items stores copies of messages that you have sent.

Deleted Items stores messages that have not yet been permanently deleted. This is similar to the Recycle Bin in Microsoft Windows or the Trash in Macintosh systems.

196

Notes:

Other Shortcuts

- In previous versions of Outlook, the My Shortcuts group was called the Mail group. You can rename the group.

- The Other Shortcuts group has shortcuts to disks and folders outside of Outlook. By default, the Other Shortcuts group has shortcuts to the My Computer icon and the Personal and Favorites folders.

- When you select a folder in the Other Shortcuts group, the contents of the disk or folder appear in the Outlook window.

- You can add to the Other Shortcuts group folder shortcuts to folders that are outside of the Outlook folders.

Use the **My Computer** icon to browse the contents of your hard disk.

When you click an icon in the Folder Bar, the contents of the drive or folder are displayed in the Outlook window.

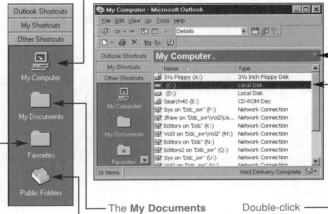

The **My Documents** folder is the default folder for documents you create.

Double-click an icon to display the contents of a drive or folder.

The **Favorites** folder stores shortcuts to your favorite Web sites.

On an intranet, use the **Public Folders** icon to open shared folders on your disk.

197

Outlook Today

Switch to Outlook Today to see your day or your week at a glance. View appointments, tasks, and mail message information all in the same window.

Notes:

- Outlook Today shows information from different Outlook components that you specify. For example, you can choose whether or not to include tasks in the display.

- You can quickly move from Outlook Today to other Outlook components by clicking icons and hyperlinks in the Outlook Today window.

1 Select **View**, **Go To**, **Outlook Today**.

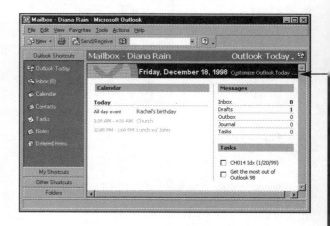

2 Click **Customize Outlook Today**. Customization options are shown in the Outlook window.

- Outlook displays information about the current week or as many days as you choose.

3 To always display the Outlook Today window whenever you start Outlook, select the **Startup** check box.

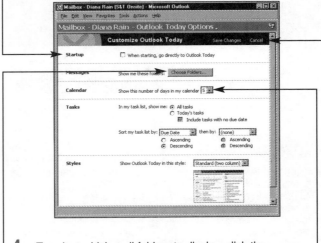

4 To select which mail folders to display, click the **Choose Folders** button Choose Folders... in the Messages area. Select each component to include and click **OK** OK .

5 Type or select the number of days to display in the Calendar area. This area of Outlook Today lists your appointments.

6 Select how Tasks should be displayed.

7 Choose from the Styles list to select a layout for the Outlook Today window.

8 Click the **Save Changes** button Save Changes or the **Cancel** button Cancel to exit. The Outlook Today window shows your customizations.

Calendar: Create an Appointment

Use Calendar to maintain an appointment book and set reminders to alert you before each appointment.

Actions ➡ 📅 New Appointment   Ctrl+N

Notes:

- If you use Outlook on a network with calendars in shared folders, you can view the schedules of other workgroup members and quickly schedule meetings by picking a time when all attendees are available.

- If you share your calendar on a network, keep it current so that other network members can rely on it.

- You can use Outlook categories to organize your appointments. For example, you might assign all appointments for a particular project to the project category.

1 Click the **New Appointment** button 📅 New or press **Ctrl+N** in the Calendar window.

OR

Click the appointment date and double-click on the time. The date and time are filled in for you in the Appointment dialog box.

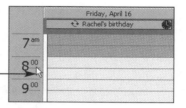

2 Type a **Subject** and **Location**.

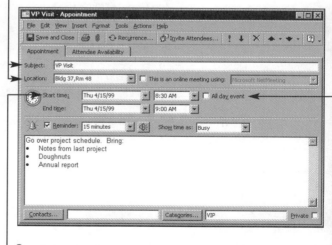

3 Select the date of the appointment in **Start time:**.

4 Click **All day event** to select. ────────

   *NOTE: When **All day event** is selected, time fields are removed from the dialog box.*

200

5 Type or select a start time and an end time.

6 Set reminder options if desired:

- To disable the reminder, click the **Reminder** check box to deselect it.
- To change the reminder time before the appointment, select the time from the **Reminder** drop-down list.
- To play a sound at the specified amount of time before the appointment, click the **Sound** button ⏻.

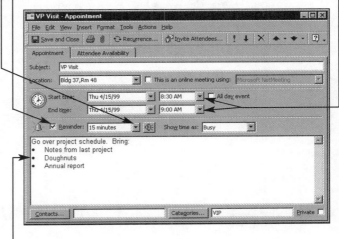

7 Type your comments in the text box.

   *NOTE: Click **Format** to change the font, align paragraphs, and add bullets in the text.*

8 Click the **Categories** button Categories... to assign one or more Outlook categories to the appointment if desired.

9 Click the **Save and Close** button Save and Close on the toolbar at the top of the window.

201

Calendar: Create a Recurring Appointment

Schedule a series of appointments that occur on a regular basis. Recurring appointments are often meetings, such as a meeting held every Friday at 2 pm. Outlook creates each individual appointment within the series and adds them all to your calendar.

Notes:

- If the recurring appointment is a meeting and you are responsible for scheduling the meeting and inviting attendees, you can set up the appointment as a meeting request. By using a meeting request rather than an appointment, you can use Outlook to send invitations to attendees.

- Creating a recurring appointment is similar to creating a regular appointment. The options are the same except that you set up the appointment date/time using the Appointment Recurrence dialog box when you create a recurring appointment.

1 Click **Actions**, **New Recurring Appointment** to display the Appointment Recurrence dialog box.

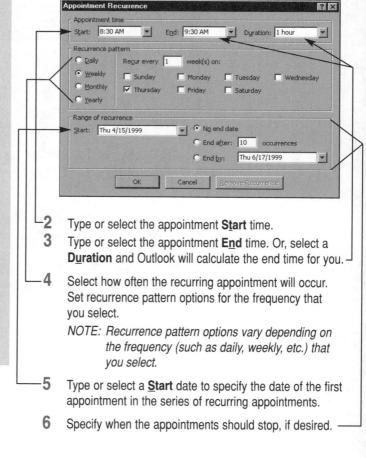

2 Type or select the appointment **Start** time.

3 Type or select the appointment **End** time. Or, select a **Duration** and Outlook will calculate the end time for you.

4 Select how often the recurring appointment will occur. Set recurrence pattern options for the frequency that you select.

NOTE: Recurrence pattern options vary depending on the frequency (such as daily, weekly, etc.) that you select.

5 Type or select a **Start** date to specify the date of the first appointment in the series of recurring appointments.

6 Specify when the appointments should stop, if desired.

Notes:

- You can edit a single instance of the recurring appointment if, for example, the meeting will be held in a different room on a particular date. Or, you can change all of the appointments in the series if the meeting room is permanently changed.

7 Click **OK** [OK] to display the Appointment dialog box. The Appointment dialog box shows the schedule for the recurring appointment.

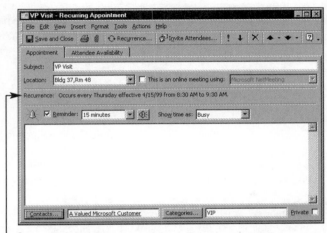

8 Set options in the Appointment dialog box as desired. Fill in fields except for start and end times, which are set in the Appointment Recurrence dialog box.

9 Click the **Save and Close** button [💾 Save and Close].

NOTE: A recurrence symbol identifies recurring appointments in the Calendar window.

↻ Usability review (Zoo room)

Calendar: Add Holidays to Your Calendar

Display the names of holidays in your Day Calendar. Holidays are a type of event—they do not change the status of your time. Your time is still shown as free for appointments.

Notes:

- If a holiday is a vacation day for you and you will be out of the office and unavailable for appointments, change the time status so that your time is shown as unavailable.

- In addition to standard holidays, Outlook flags important days that are not regarded as holidays, such as Tax Day (April 15th).

1 Click **Tools**, **Options** to open the Options dialog box.

2 Click the **Calendar Options** button Calendar Options... to open the Calendar Options dialog box.

3 Click the **Add Holidays** button Add Holidays... . The Add Holidays to Calendar dialog box appears.

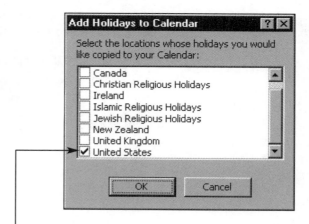

4 Click the holidays you wish to add to your calendar. You can add multiple categories if desired.

5 Click **OK** OK .

Outlook imports the specified holiday file(s) and redisplays the Calendar Options dialog box.

6 Click **OK** OK twice to close dialog boxes.

Edit a Holiday

1   Display the day on which the holiday appears.

   NOTE: To go to a particular date, press Ctrl+G. Type or select the day to go to.

2   Double-click the holiday banner to open the Event dialog box.

3   Change options as desired.

4   Click the **Save and Close** button.

Remove a Holiday from Your Calendar

1   Display the day on which the holiday appears.

   NOTE: To go to a particular date, press Ctrl+G. Type or select the day to go to.

2   Right-click the holiday banner to open the shortcut menu.

   NOTE: The banner is the title of the holiday.

3   Click **Delete**.

Calendar: Print a Weekly or Monthly Schedule

Print your schedule for entire weeks or months. Use Day/Week/Month view and Weekly style or Monthly style to create this kind of report.

Notes:

- Print a calendar containing a specified number of weeks or months. You can print one or two weeks or months per page.

- You can include the TaskPad in your report and an area in which to write notes on each page of your calendar.

1 Click **View**, **Go To**, **Calendar** to switch to Calendar.

2 Click **View**, **Current View**, **Day/Week/Month** to switch to Day/Week/Month view if necessary.

3 Click the **Print** button or press **Ctrl+P** to display the Print dialog box.

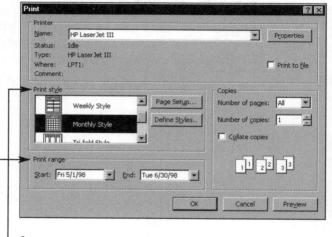

4 Select **Weekly Style** or **Monthly Style** in the **Print style** list.

5 Set **Start** and **End** dates in the **Print range** boxes to specify the range of weeks or months.

6 Click the **Page Setup** button. The Page Setup dialog box opens.

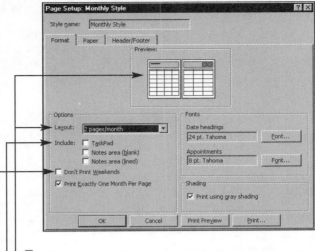

7 Select a **Layout** option to specify whether one month or one week should be printed on one page or two. The Preview box shows a sample of the layout that you select.

8 Select other information that you would like to include in the report, if desired.

NOTE: Adding the TaskPad and/or Notes area takes up extra space on the page. Preview your report to make sure it is not too cluttered to be useful.

9 Specify whether or not you want to include weekends in the report.

10 Set any options specific to the style of report that you have chosen.

NOTE: These options vary depending on the style you are using. Use Print Preview to see the effect of options that you select. To see a pop-up explanation of an option, click ? in the corner of the dialog box and then click the option.

11 Use the **Paper** tab to change the paper size, if desired.

12 Modify headers and footers, if desired.

13 Click the **Print Preview** button | Print Preview | to view the report.

14 Click the **Print** button | Print... | in the Page Setup dialog box or the **Print** button | 🖨 Print... | in Print Preview to return to the Print dialog box.

15 Click | OK | to print.

207

Calendar: Set Reminder Options

Specify the initial settings for reminder options in the Appointment dialog box and the Recurring Appointment dialog box. You can change reminder options for individual appointments when you create or edit an appointment.

Notes:

- This procedure determines how reminder options are set in new appointments. For example, when you install Outlook, it is set to display reminders 15 minutes before appointments. You might want to change this to 5 minutes before appointments— or you can disable reminders altogether.

1 Click **Tools**, **Options** to open the Options dialog box.

2 To disable reminders, click the **Default reminder** check box to clear it.

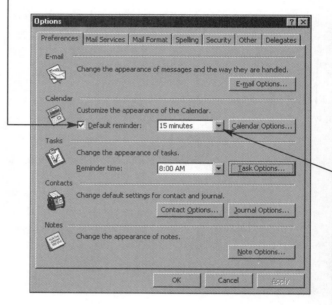

3 To change the reminder time before the appointment, select the time interval from the drop-down list box.

4 To turn the reminder sound or the Reminder dialog box on or off, if desired:

a. Click the **Other** tab.

b. Click the **Advanced Options** button [Advanced Options...]. The Advanced Options dialog box opens.

c. Click the **Reminder Options** button [Reminder Options...]. The Reminder Options dialog box opens.

Notes:

- In addition to setting the reminder time before appointments, you can also disable the reminder sound or the Reminder dialog box. The Reminder dialog box pops up at the time set for the reminder. By default, Outlook displays the Reminder dialog box and plays a sound when the reminder is due.

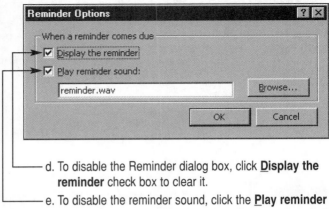

d. To disable the Reminder dialog box, click **Display the reminder** check box to clear it.

e. To disable the reminder sound, click the **Play reminder sound** check box to clear it.

f. To play a different sound for reminders, type the pathname of the sound file you want to play or click the **Browse** button [Browse...] to select the sound file.

g. Click **OK** [OK] twice to return to the Options dialog box.

5 Click **OK** [OK] to close the Options dialog box.

Notes:

- If you have set a reminder for an appointment, the Reminder dialog box pops up on your screen before the appointment. You need to respond to the reminder by selecting an option in the dialog box.

- If your computer was off when the reminder was scheduled to appear, Outlook displays the Overdue dialog box, which has the same options as the Reminder dialog box.

Respond to a Reminder

Select an option in the Reminder dialog box.

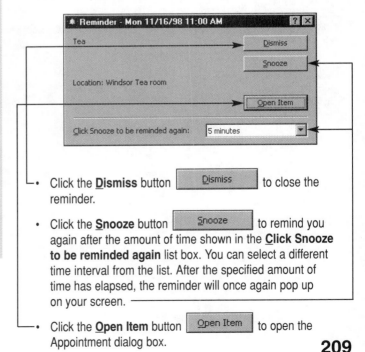

- Click the **Dismiss** button [Dismiss] to close the reminder.

- Click the **Snooze** button [Snooze] to remind you again after the amount of time shown in the **Click Snooze to be reminded again** list box. You can select a different time interval from the list. After the specified amount of time has elapsed, the reminder will once again pop up on your screen.

- Click the **Open Item** button [Open Item] to open the Appointment dialog box.

209

Contacts: Add a Contact

Enter address, phone number, e-mail address, and other information about a contact. A contact is one person or business.

Notes:

- You can include an extension in a phone number, for example: 555-5555 x439. Precede the extension with "x" or "Ext." so that Outlook ignores the extension when autodialing.

- Start international phone numbers with the country code.

- If you include a phone number, a fax number, and/or an e-mail address, Outlook adds the contact to the Address Book. You can quickly send a fax or address a mail message by selecting the contact from the Address Book.

1 Click the **New Contact** button or press **Ctrl+N** in the Contacts window.

OR

Click **File**, **New**, **Contact** or press **Ctrl+Shift+C** from anywhere in Outlook.
The Contact dialog box opens.

2 Click the **Full Name** button Full Name... . The Check Full Name dialog box opens.

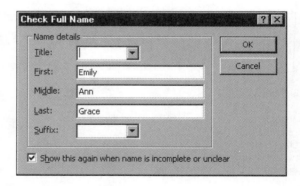

3 Type first, last, title, and other name information.

4 Click **OK** OK . The name that you added has been entered in the Contact dialog box.

210

• If you assign a category to a contact, you can arrange contacts by category in the Contacts window and organize journal entries for contacts by category.

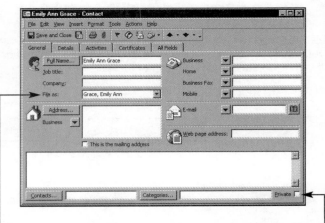

5 Enter contact information in the Contact dialog box. Most fields are self-explanatory. Here are some tips:

• Select the name under which you want to file the contact in **File as**. Outlook files contacts by this information so what you select here determines the letter under which the contact will be stored.

• Click the drop-down arrow ▼ under the **Address** button to select another address type to enter (such as Home address). You can enter as many as three addresses.

• Click the drop-down arrow ▼ next to one of the phone numbers and select a phone type (such as home fax, page, car, etc.) to enter more phone numbers.

• Select **Private** if you want to hide the contact in public folders when other people have access to your contact information.

• Click the **Categories** button Categories... to assign one or more categories to the contact.

6 Use the other tabs in the dialog box to enter more information. For example, the Details tab includes fields for personal information about the contact, such as birthday or anniversary dates.

7 Click the **Save and Close** button ⊟ Save and Close .

OR

Click the **Save** button to save the contact and add another contact.

Contacts: Call a Contact

Use AutoDial to have Outlook dial the phone number of a contact for you. Outlook can automatically create a journal entry to record information about the phone call, such as the contact name and the length of the call.

Notes:

- Your computer must have a modem to dial from Outlook.

- If you use a switching device to use fax, modem, and voice mail on one line, this procedure will not work unless the switcher allows you to switch to voice mode after dialing.

- You can autodial phone numbers in the speed dial list from anywhere in Outlook. To dial other numbers, you must be in Contacts.

1 Select the contact you want to call in the Contacts window.

Click the **New Call** button 🕮 ▾ on the toolbar.

OR

Press **Ctrl+Shift+D** from anywhere in Outlook to call a contact in the speed dial list.

2 Before dialing, set options in the New Call dialog box if necessary:

a. Select the contact you want to call if using the speed dial list.

NOTE: *If you selected the contact in the Contacts window, this field is filled in for you.*

b. Select the phone number you want to call if multiple phone numbers are available for the contact.

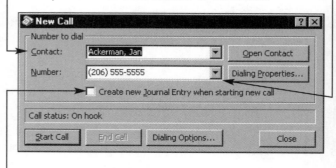

c. Select **Create new Journal Entry** if you want to record information about the call in a journal entry.

Notes:

- After Outlook has dialed the phone number, you can disconnect at any time by clicking the **Hang Up** button

  `Hang Up` .

- If you created a journal entry for the call, Outlook starts the timer after dialing. You can stop the clock at any time by clicking the **Pause Timer** button

  `Pause Timer` .

  To resume, click the **Start Timer** button

  `Start Timer` .

d. To view information about the contact in the Contact dialog box, click the **Open Contact** button

`Open Contact` .

e. To set properties specific to the call, such as calling card information and how to access an outside line from your current location, click the **Dialing Properties** button `Dialing Properties...` .

f. To set options for contacts in the speed dial list, click the **Dialing Options** button `Dialing Options...` .

3 Click the **Start Call** button `Start Call` to dial the number.

4 Pick up the phone receiver. Then click the **Talk** button `Talk` . You can now speak into the receiver.

5 When finished with the call, hang up the phone.

6 Click the **New Call** button `New Call` in the Windows taskbar to display the New Call dialog box.

7 Click the **End Call** button `End Call` to stop the timer.

8 If Outlook created a journal entry for the call, click the **Save and Close** button `Save and Close` in the journal entry.

Redial a Contact

1 In the Contacts window, click **Actions**, **Call Contact**, **Redial**.

2 Select the number you want to dial.

3 Follow the previous procedure from step 3.

Notes:

- Outlook stores the phone numbers that you last autodialed. To redial a contact quickly, use this procedure to select a number from a list of recently dialed phone numbers.

Contacts: Get Driving Directions

Open the Microsoft Expedia Maps Web site and display a map showing the address of the current contact. From that page, you can go to another Web page that will give you driving directions to the contact address.

Notes:

- You must have Internet Explorer installed and you must have Internet service for this procedure to work. When you display a map, Internet Explorer starts up and connects to the Web. It searches Microsoft Expedia Maps for the contact address and displays it.

1 In the Contact window, double-click the contact you want to open. The Contact dialog box opens.

2 Click **Actions**, **Display Map of Address** in the Contact dialog box.

OR

Click the **Display Map of Address** button.

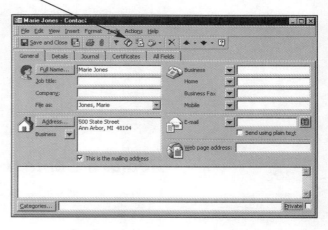

Internet Explorer starts and displays the Microsoft Expedia Web site with the map for the contact address.

214

- While you are at the Web site, you can look up and get driving directions to a different address. The Expedia site has addresses nationwide.

3 Use the Web page to get the information you need:

- Click the **change search** link to search for a different address and enter the address you want to find.
- Use the Zoom Level tools to enlarge the map and show more detail or to move out from the map and show more of the area surrounding the address.

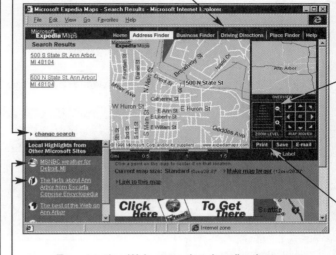

- To go to other Web pages that describe the town or location of the address, click a link in the Local Highlights column.
- To print the page, click the **Print** button Print .
- For detailed instructions that will get you from an address that you specify to the contact address, click the **Driving directions** button Driving directions .

4 When finished, to exit Internet Explorer, click **File**, **Close**.

Contacts: Maintain a Speed Dial List

Create a list of the phone numbers that you most frequently call using the Outlook autodial feature. You can have Outlook call a contact in the speed dial list from anywhere in Outlook. You do not have to return to the Contact window to dial the number.

Notes:

- Each entry in the speed dial list can consist of one contact name and one phone number. To add multiple phone numbers for a contact to the list, you must create a separate entry for each phone number.

1 Press **Ctrl+Shift+D**. The New Call dialog box opens.

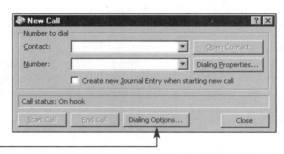

2 Click the **Dialing Options** button `Dialing Options...`. The Dialing Options dialog box opens. This dialog box contains the speed dial list.

3 Type the contact name in the **Name** field.

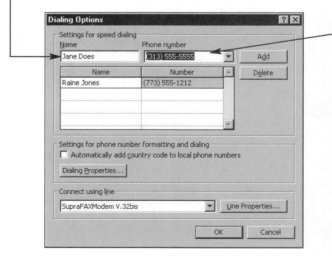

4 Press **Tab** to move to the **Phone number** field. Outlook displays the default phone number(s) for this contact.

Notes:

- Outlook adds the speed dial list to the **Actions**, **Call Contact**, **Speed Dial** menu.

5 If there are multiple phone numbers for this contact and you would like to add a different number than the one

displayed, click the **Phone number** drop-down arrow to select the number.

NOTE: To add multiple phone numbers for a single contact, create a new entry in the list for each phone number.

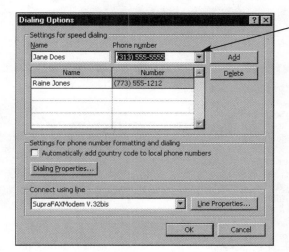

6 Click the **Add** button [Add] to add the contact to the list.

7 Repeat steps 3-6 to add more contacts to the speed dial list if desired.

8 Click **OK** [OK].

9 Click the **Close** button [Close] in the New Call dialog box.

E-Mail: Create a Personal Distribution List

By creating and naming a distribution list of multiple e-mail and fax addresses, you can send the same mail to an entire group of recipients.

Notes:

- Create a personal distribution list when you often send the same mail message to the same group of individuals. For example, you might create a group for the members of your workgroup, a team of employees who are all working on a particular project, a group of friends who often meet for lunch, etc.

- In previous versions of Outlook, you used a Personal Address Book or a group distribution list. These have been replaced in Outlook 2000 with personal distribution lists. You can import your Personal Address Book to use it in Outlook 2000.

1 Select **File**, **New**, **Distribution List**. The Distribution List dialog box opens.

2 Type a name for the new distribution list. (*Examples:* Lunch Bunch, Editors, X Project)

3 To add members that are not listed in your address book or contact list:

a. Click the **Add New** button [Add New...]. The Add New Member dialog box opens.

b. Type the name that will appear in the distribution list in the **Display Name** text box.

c. Enter the **E-mail address** and select an **Address type**.

NOTE: This option is not available if Outlook is configured to use only one form of e-mail (such as Internet only or Exchange only).

d. To add the person to your contact list, if desired, select **Add to contacts**.

e. Click **OK** | OK |.

4 To select members of the group from your contacts list or address book:

a. Click the **Select Members** button | Select Members... |. The Select Members dialog box opens.

b. Select the address book or contacts list you want to see.

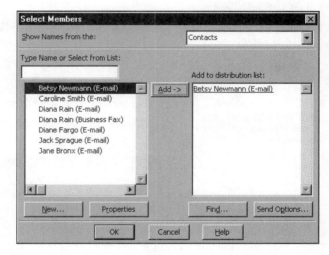

c. Select contact(s) to add to the distribution list. To select multiple names, press **Ctrl** while you click each name.

d. Click the **Add** button | Add -> |. The selected names are added to the list.

e. Click **OK** | OK | to return to the Distribution List dialog box.

5 Click the **Save and Close** button | 🖫 Save and Close | to save the distribution list and close the dialog box.

219

E-Mail: Create and Send a Mail Message

Create a new mail message. Select one or more recipients from an address book and then send the message.

Notes:

- Outlook will transmit messages over the network according to the message delivery settings you choose. You may set up Outlook to send messages immediately or to wait until you issue the command to send and receive all messages.

1 Click the **New Mail Message** button 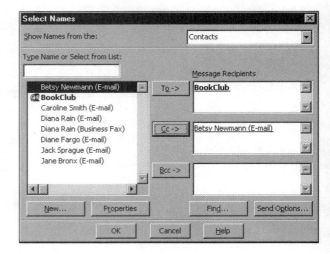 or press **Ctrl+N** from the Mail window.

OR

Click **File**, **New**, **Mail Message** or press **Ctrl+Shift+M** from anywhere in Outlook.

The Message dialog box opens.

2 Click the **To...** button to select the message recipient(s). The Select Names dialog box opens.

NOTE: You can type recipient names rather than selecting them. Skip to step 4 if you type the names.

3 To select message recipient(s):

a. Click the 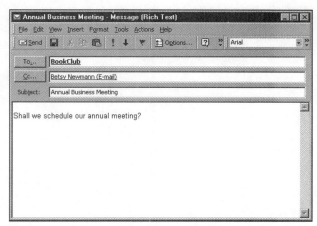 drop-down arrow and select a different address book, if desired.

b. Click recipient name(s).
   *NOTE: To select multiple names, press **Ctrl** and click next name.*

c. Click the **To** button To -> to add selected names as recipients.

   OR

   Click the **Carbon Copy** button Cc -> to add selected names as Carbon Copy recipients

   OR

   Click the **Blind Carbon Copy** button Bcc -> to add selected names as Blind Carbon Copy recipients.

d. Repeat from step a. to add more recipients, if desired.

e. Click **OK** OK . Outlook displays the Message dialog box.

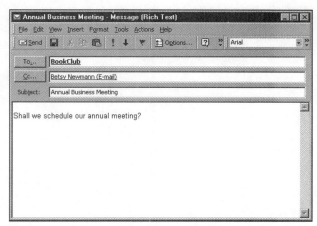

4 Type a **Subject**.

5 Type the text of the message.

6 Click the **Send** button Send to send the message.

E-Mail: Forward a Mail Message

When you receive a mail message, you can send a copy of the message on to someone else. You can also add a comment when you forward the message.

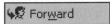

1   Open the message you want to forward.

2   Click the **Forward** button .

The message title is added to the top of the message preceded by "FW:" so that recipients can see that this is a forwarded message.

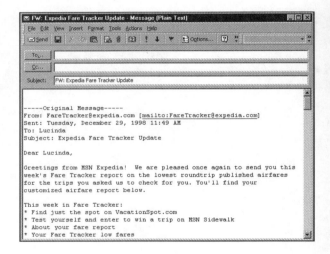

3   Type recipient(s) you want to forward the mail to.

OR

Click the **To...** button ⬚ To... to open the Select Names dialog box, and select recipients. For help selecting recipients in the Select Names dialog box, see *Create and Send a Mail Message.*

4   Type your comments as desired.

5   Click the **Send** button ⬚ Send.

- When you send a mail message, you can reroute any replies to your message to another E-mail address. For example, if you know that you will be at a different computer with a different mail account, you can make sure you receive responses to an important message by specifying that responses be sent to that account. Or, it might be that you have designated someone else to handle them.

- You can have replies sent to multiple addresses. For example, if you have two mail accounts, you could have replies sent to both accounts.

- You cannot reroute replies to a group distribution list.

Automatically Forward Responses to a Message

1   Create the message.

2   Click the **Message Options** dialog button [:: Options...].
The Message Options dialog box opens.

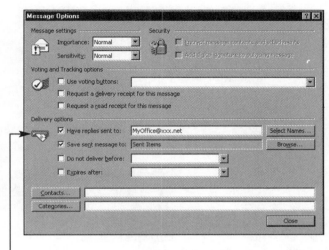

3   Click the **Have replies sent to** check box to select it.
Outlook enters your current e-mail address in the text box.

NOTE: You can have the message forwarded to multiple addresses. You could keep your current e-mail address and add another address so that replies are sent to all addresses.

NOTE: If the names exceed the width of the box, use the Left or Right Arrow key to scroll.

4   Type the e-mail address to which you want to send replies automatically.

OR

If the address to which you want to send is listed in your address book, click the **Select Names** button

[Select Names...] to select the address.

5   Click the **Close** button [Close].

6   Finish creating the message and click the **Send** button

[:: Send].

223

E-Mail: Send a File with a Mail Message

Send a file when you send a mail message. The attached file appears as an icon in the message. The recipient can double-click the icon to open the file or right-click the icon to display a shortcut menu.

Notes:

- You can send multiple files in a single mail message. Each file is represented by an icon in the message window.

- The recipient can double-click the file icon to open the file. This opens the program in which the file was created—for example, Microsoft Word. If the recipient does not have the program installed, Outlook suggests which program to use to open the file.

1   Position cursor in the mail message text box where you want the icon representing the attached file to appear.

2   Click **Insert**, **File** or click the **Insert File** button. The Insert File dialog box opens.

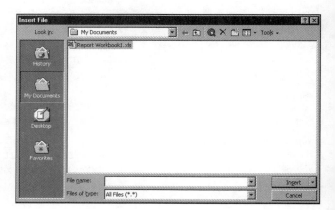

3   Use the **Look in** list to open the folder containing the file you want to send.

- The file is saved as part of the mail message. The recipient can open the file and save it as a separate file (using the **File, Save Attachments** command in the message). Otherwise, the file is deleted with the mail message.

- The recipient can save the file without opening it by right-clicking on the icon and selecting **Save As**.

4 Select the file and click the **Insert** button [Insert ▼].
The file is added to the mail message.

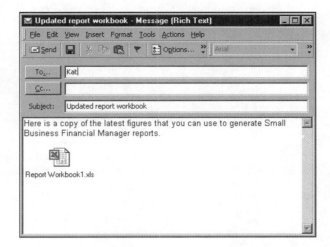

5 Repeat from step 2 to attach other files, if desired.

6 Finish creating the mail message and click the **Send** button [✉ Send].

NOTE: To remove an attached file, right-click on the file icon and click Remove.

Journal: Create a Journal Entry

A journal entry stores information about a single activity. Use this procedure to manually create a journal entry for activities that Outlook cannot automatically record for you.

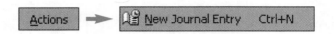

Notes:

- Although Outlook can automatically create journal entries for activities that you perform on your computer, such as working in a file or sending a mail message, you must manually create entries for some types of activities. For example, you might create an entry if you read a printed report and are tracking billable activities.

- You can have Outlook time the activity for you if you create the journal entry when you start the activity. You can pause and resume the timer while timing an activity if you are temporarily called away from the task.

1　Click the **New Journal Entry** button 🕮 New or press **Ctrl+N** in the Journal window.

OR

Press **Ctrl+Shift+J** from anywhere in Outlook.
The Journal Entry dialog box opens.

2　Type a **Subject** to describe the entry.

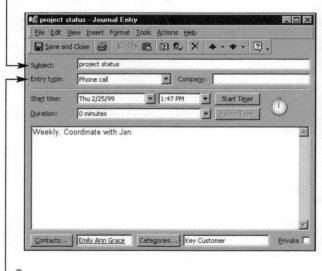

3　Select an **Entry type**.

4　If the activity has a contact associated with it, type the contact name or click the **Contacts** button ⎴Contacts...⎴ and select from the contact list.

5　Enter notes or a description as desired.

6　If you use Outlook categories, click the **Categories** button ⎴Categories...⎴ and select one or more categories.

Notes:

- If you assign
  categories to
  journal entries, you
  can view journal
  entries grouped
  by categories.

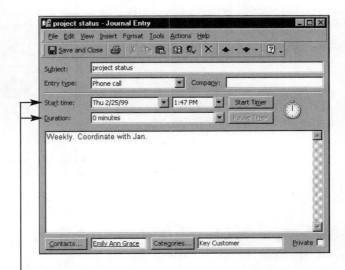

7   If you are recording an activity that you have already
timed, enter a **Start time** and **Duration**. Then click the

Save and Close button <kbd>Save and Close</kbd>.

OR

To time the activity:

a. Click the **Start Timer** button <kbd>Start Timer</kbd>.

b. Perform the activity.

c. If you are temporarily called away from the activity,

   click the **Pause Timer** button <kbd>Pause Timer</kbd> to
   pause the timer. Then, click the **Start Timer** button

   <kbd>Start Timer</kbd> to restart the timer when you are
   ready to resume.

d. When finished, click the **Save and Close** button

   <kbd>Save and Close</kbd>. Outlook stops the timer and
   enters in the **Duration** field the amount of time the
   activity took.

227

Journal: Create Automatic Journal Entries

An automatic journal entry is a record of an activity that involves your computer. Sending a task request, receiving a mail message, and working in a Microsoft Word document are all activities that Outlook can record for you. Outlook creates automatic journal entries for the activities that you specify.

Notes:

- This procedure sets the default automatic journal settings. You can change them on individual items. For example, when you send a mail message, you can specify whether or not to create an automatic journal entry for the message.

- Edit automatic journal entries to add relevant information such as a category or notes.

1 Click **Tools**, **Options** to open the Options dialog box.

2 Click the **Journal Options** button Journal Options... to open the Journal Options dialog box, which lists activities that you can record automatically.

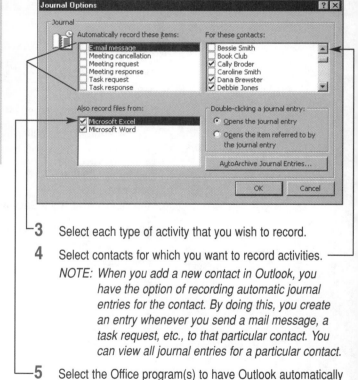

3 Select each type of activity that you wish to record.

4 Select contacts for which you want to record activities.

   NOTE: When you add a new contact in Outlook, you have the option of recording automatic journal entries for the contact. By doing this, you create an entry whenever you send a mail message, a task request, etc., to that particular contact. You can view all journal entries for a particular contact.

5 Select the Office program(s) to have Outlook automatically create journal entries whenever you work in documents created in a program.

6 Click **OK** OK twice to close dialog boxes.

Continue →

Tasks: Create a Recurring Task

A recurring task is a series of repeating action items. Examples of recurring tasks might be submitting a status report every two weeks or calling a contact every six months. You need only create a single recurring task; Outlook will take care of creating the next tasks as needed.

Notes:

- Outlook creates two types of recurring tasks:

  1. Tasks based on a pattern of specific dates, such as every other Friday or the third Saturday of each month. When a recurring task falls due, Outlook calculates the next due date and creates the next recurring task.

  2. Tasks that depend on the completion of the previous task. Outlook creates the next recurring task when you mark the current task as complete. The date on which you mark the task as complete is the date used to calculate the due date for the next recurring task. For example, if you call a particular client every three months, you don't want to schedule the next call until you actually contact the client.

1 Click the **New Task** button or press **Ctrl+N** from the Task window to display the Task dialog box.

2 Type a **Subject** for the task. The subject appears as the title in the task list.

3 Click the **Task Recurrence** button to display the Task Recurrence dialog box.

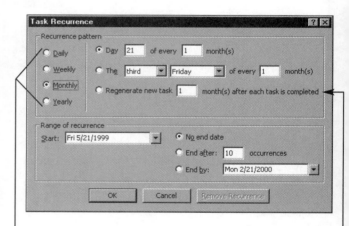

4 Select the frequency at which the task will recur.

   NOTE: The options that you will use to set up the recurrence schedule vary depending on the frequency that you select. This example shows the options for a Monthly recurrence pattern.

5 Specify the kind of recurring task you want to create:

   Click **Regenerate new task** to create a recurrence pattern dependent on the completion of the previous task. Outlook creates the first recurring task on the due date that you provide.

   OR

Set options for selected frequency to automatically create a new task at the specified time interval. ⎯⎯⎯

NOTE: Recurrence pattern options vary depending on selected frequency.

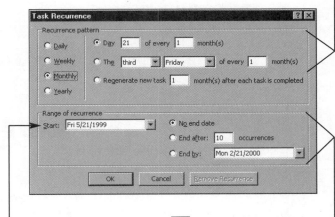

6 Type a **Start** date or click to select from Date Navigator calendar.

*NOTE: Outlook creates the first in the series of recurring tasks on the specified **Start** date.*

7 Select a date when Outlook will stop creating recurring tasks, if desired. You can specify that the task stop on a certain date or after a specified number of occurrences. ⎯

*NOTE: If **Regenerate new task** is selected, you cannot set an **End by** date.*

Notes:

- You might need to skip an individual task in a series of recurring tasks—for example, if the task is to write a monthly newsletter that is not published in January. In that case, you would skip the task for January.

- Outlook deletes the task and creates the next recurring task.

- You cannot skip a task that uses a recurrence pattern dependent on the completion of a task. In order for Outlook to create the next task, you must mark the current task as complete.

8 Click **OK** to return to the Task dialog box.

*NOTE: In the Task dialog box, the **Due** date is set to the next occurrence of the task.*

9 Set other fields in the Task dialog box, if desired. See *Create a Task*.

NOTE: Do not change date fields; these are set up according to the recurrence pattern.

10 Click the **Save and Close** button.

Skip a Recurring Task

1 Open the recurring task.

2 Click **Actions**, **Skip Occurrence**.

3 Click the **Save and Close** button.

231

Tasks: Create a Task

A task is a single action item that must be completed either by a particular date or by an unspecified time. Create a task for each action item within a project. Then you can track the task's progress until its completion.

Notes:

- Tasks are also visible in the TaskPad in Calendar.

- Tasks that are past due (not marked complete on the due date) appear in red in the task list.

- You can have Outlook display a reminder at a specified date and time.

- The Owner is the person who is currently responsible for the task. You cannot edit this field.

1 Click the **New Task** button or press **Ctrl+N** in the Task window.

OR

Click **File**, **New**, **Task** or press **Ctrl+Shift+K** from anywhere in Outlook.

The Task dialog box opens.

2 Type a description in **Subject**. The subject will appear in the Task window task list and the TaskPad in Calendar.

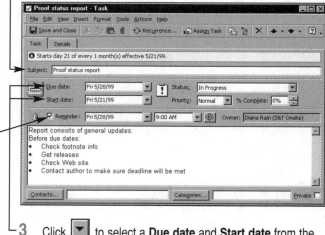

3 Click ▼ to select a **Due date** and **Start date** from the Date Navigator pop-up calendar.

NOTE: If a date does not apply, click the **None** button

None in the Date Navigator calendar.

4 To have Outlook display and/or sound a reminder:

a. Click **Reminder** to select (enable reminder) or deselect (disable the reminder) it.

b. If the reminder is enabled, select the date and time you want Outlook to display and/or sound it.

c. Click the **Sound** button to set the reminder sound to play. In the Reminder Sound dialog box, select **Play this sound** to play a reminder sound or deselect it to turn off the sound. You can change the sound that will play. Click **OK** OK .

5 If you have started the task, select an option from the **Status:** list box. You can also specify the percentage of the task that has been completed.

6 Select High, Normal, or Low **Priority**.

7 Type your comments in the text box. Click **Format** to change the font, change the paragraph alignment, or add bullets, if desired.

8 Click the **Categories** button Categories... to assign one or more categories to the task, if desired.

9 Select **Private** in the lower-right corner of the dialog box to hide the task in shared folders, if desired.

─10 Click the **Details** tab to display more options.

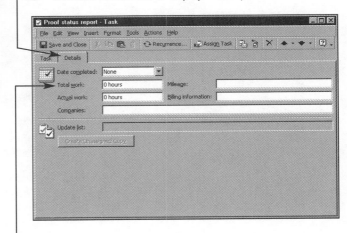

─11 Type number of hours the task is expected to take in **Total work**.

NOTE: Outlook converts hours to days or weeks when you save the task.

12 Type mileage, billing, contact, and company information, if desired.

13 Click the **Save and Close** button Save and Close .

233

Integration

Each of the Office tools can be used separately, or they can be used together to produce professional looking documents. For example, a report prepared in Word can be enhanced with charts and graphs created in Excel or slides created in PowerPoint. Because Microsoft Office is designed to have all the components working together, integrating the separate applications can be easily done.

Windowing Files from Different Applications

Microsoft Office allows you to work with several files simultaneously—the files can all be from the same application or they can be from different applications. For example, you can move between an opened Word document and an Excel workbook.

Notes:

- The exact number of files that can be used at once depends on how much memory your computer has.

- When you begin a new application, Office provides a full-screen or maximized window for your work.

1 To minimize a window, click the **Minimize** button  on the upper-right hand corner of the Menu bar.

2 The minimized file will be become a button on the taskbar at the bottom of the screen.

3 By clicking on the button, you can access the open file in the program that it was created in.

OR

If you wish to view the files from several programs at the same time:

1 Right-click on the Taskbar on the bottom of your screen.

2 Select the view option you prefer. You may **Cascade**, **Tile Horizontally**, or **Tile Vertically**.

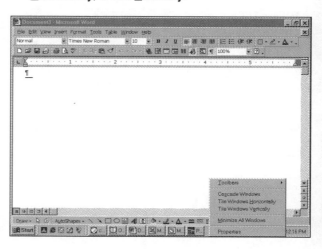

NOTE: If you are copying sections from a document in one application to a document in another application, cascading your files is a convenient way to work.

Export an Access Database to an Excel File

You may wish to use an Excel workbook to summarize and analyze information saved in an Access database. This can be accomplished by exporting, or sending, data from Access to Excel.

Tools → Office Links → Analyze It with MS Excel

Notes:

- Exporting is used if you wish to create a new workbook file from a database.

1 Open the Access file that you want to export.

2 Select (highlight) the table.

3 Click **Tools**, **Office Links**, **Analyze It with MS Excel**.

4 The database table opens in Excel.

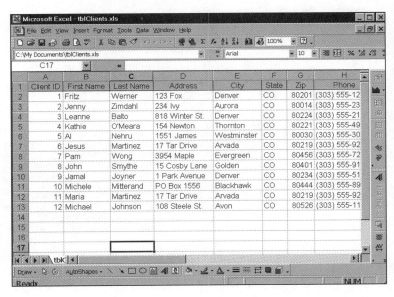

5 Save and name the worksheet file.

Export a PowerPoint Presentation into a Word Document

You can include a complete PowerPoint presentation in a Word document so that the slides may be viewed one at a time.

Notes:

- If you wish to bring only one slide into a Word document, you can use the **Copy**, **Paste Special**, **Paste** link procedure. When you use this procedure, the data will be linked.

1 Open the PowerPoint Presentation that you wish to export into Word.

2 Select **File**, **Send To**, **Microsoft Word**.

- You must be in Slide Sorter view to copy a single slide.

3 Select the desired layout option from the Write-Up dialog box.

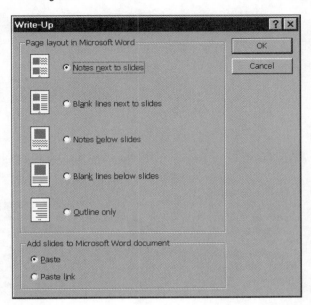

4 If desired, select the **Paste link** option. If this option is selected, then you can double-click on the PowerPoint object in Word and PowerPoint toolbars and menus will become visible.

5 Click **OK**   OK   .

Export Information from Outlook to other Office Programs

This procedure allows you to export Outlook files for use in another application.

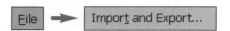

1 Click **File**, **Import and Export**.

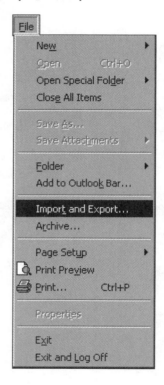

2 Click **Export to a file** from the **Choose an action to perform list**, and then click the **Next** button Next > .

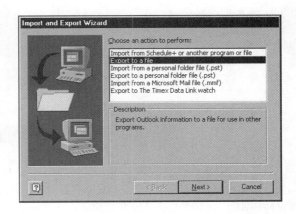

3 **Select folder to export from**, and then click the **Next** button | Next > |.

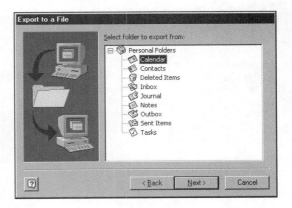

4 Select what type of file you wish to create, and then click the **Next** button | Next > |.

5 Type name of what you want to **Save exported file as** or click the **Browse** button | Browse... |. Then, click the **Next** button | Next > |.

6 The Export to a File dialog box appears noting the action that you are about to perform. Click the **Finish** button | Finish | to begin the export procedure.

Integrate an Excel Worksheet File and a Word Document

An Excel chart or worksheet can add supporting or visual documentation to a Word document.

Notes:

- The File that you are taking the data from is called the source file and the file that is receiving the data is the destination file. For example, if you are integrating an Excel chart into a report that was created in Word, the Excel file would be the source file and the Word file would be the destination file.

1 Open the Excel source file.

2 Highlight the worksheet or chart area that you wish to copy.

3 Click **Edit**, **Copy** or **Ctrl+C**.

4 Open the Word file (destination file) and place your insertion point at the location where you wish to insert the source file.

5 Click **Edit**, **Paste Special**. The Paste Special dialog box appears.

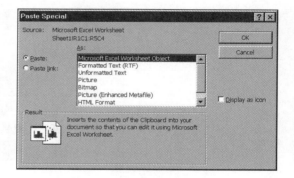

6 Select **Microsoft Excel Worksheet Object** in the **As** list box.

7 If desired, click **Paste link**. If this option is selected, the object in the destination file will be automatically updated if any edits or changes are made to the source file.

8 Click **OK**.

> NOTE: Using the **Paste**, **Paste Special** procedure allows you to make edits to the chart or worksheet in Word without changing the source material. When the chart is double-clicked, Excel menus and toolbars appear. You can then return to the Word document by clicking outside the Excel object.

Index

EXCEL

ACCESS

E

J

O

T

U

INTEGRATION

E

I

W

Notes

Notes

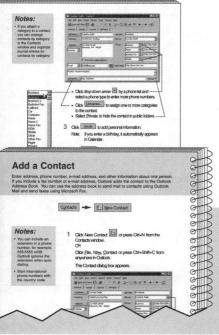

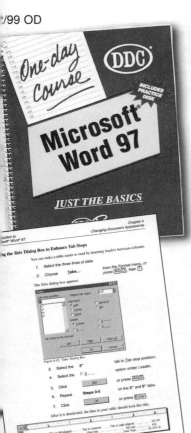

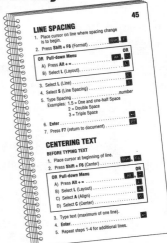

MOUS

Microsoft® initiated the **MOUS (Microsoft® Office User Specialist) program** to provide Office users a means of demo strating their level of proficiency in each application in the Offic suite. After the successful completion of the certification test in an application, users receive a certificate that reflects their leve of proficiency.

The **MOUS program** establishes the criteria for both proficient and expert levels in Word, Excel, PowerPoint, FrontPage, and Access, and proficient skill levels in Outlook.

Tests are given at Authorized Testing Centers around the country. Each test takes about 45 minutes to complete.

For more information on how you can become MOUS certified, visit our Web site!
www.ddcpub.com